D1191869

JOURNAL FOR THE STUDY OF THE OLD TESTAMENT
SUPPLEMENT SERIES
24

Editors
David J A Clines
Philip R Davies
David M Gunn

Department of Biblical Studies
The University of Sheffield
Sheffield S10 2TN
England

MIDIAN, MOAB AND EDOM

The History and Archaeology
of Late Bronze and Iron Age Jordan
and North-West Arabia

Edited by
JOHN F.A. SAWYER
AND DAVID J.A. CLINES

Journal for the Study of the Old Testament
Supplement Series, 24

Sheffield 1983

Published by
JSOT Press
Department of Biblical Studies
University of Sheffield
Sheffield S10 2TN

Printed in Great Britain by Redwood Burn Ltd.,
Trowbridge, Wiltshire.
1983

British Library Cataloguing in Publication Data

Midian, Moab and Edom.--(Journal for the study of the
    Old Testament supplement series ISSN 0309-0787;24)
    1. Bronze age--Jordan   2. Jordan--Antiquities
    I. Sawyer, John F. A.   II. Clines, David J. A.
    III. Series
    933   GN778.4.J/

    ISBN 0-905774-48-5
    ISBN 0-905774-49-3 Pbk

C O N T E N T S

PREFACE

The great additions which have been made during the past ten years or so to our knowledge of the archaeology and early history of the country east of the Jordan river were convincingly demonstrated at the International Conference on the Archaeology of Jordan held in Oxford in March 1980. At the Conference a theme which recurred in a number of papers was that of the situation in East Jordan at that crucial period at the end of the 2nd millennium BC and the beginning of the 1st - the terminal Late Bronze Age and the initial Iron Age - when, in neighbouring Palestine and Syria, and in countries further afield as well, great changes were taking place in the political, economic and demographic scene. My own contribution consisted of some suggestions concerning possible contacts between East Jordan and its southerly neighbour, Arabia, at about this time, and had to do in part with certain evidence which - as I believed - related to the people known in the Old Testament as the Midianites. The Midianites are not among the best known of ancient Near Eastern peoples, though their probable connection with the Arabian trade routes, with the early exploitation of the camel and with copper metallurgy, as well as their relevance to the Biblical exodus and conquest narratives, make them of more than passing interest. Research on the Midianites and related groups such as the Edomites has in fact grown in recent years; and in the course of informal discussions during the Oxford Conference (particularly with Dr John Bartlett of Trinity College, Dublin, Dr John Sawyer of the University of Newcastle, and Miss Elizabeth Payne, a research student of the same university) the idea was mooted of another, smaller, colloquium at which some of the recent work relating to the subject could be considered in greater detail. The idea found ready acceptance, and the task of arranging such a meeting was taken in hand. The Colloquium was held at the University of London Institute of Archaeology on 3-4 April 1981 and was attended by approximately fifty scholars, from America, Europe and the Near East, as well as from Britain. The papers delivered reflected admirably the wide range of approaches - textual, linguistic, archaeological, anthropological, technological - which modern research has adopted towards investigating the problems concerned. Those papers for which the authors submitted manuscripts are herewith published, and will, it is hoped, serve not only as a progress report on the research in question but also as a testimony to the academic stimulus provided by the Oxford Conference.

Peter J. Parr

7

EXCAVATIONS AT BUSEIRAH (BIBLICAL BOZRAH)

Crystal-M. Bennett
British Institute at Amman for Archaeology and History
Amman, JORDAN

With the finding of a seal impression of Qos Gabr in the small village settlement on the top of Umm al Biyara, a mountain overlooking Petra from the west, it was evident that the existing ruins at modern Buseirah should be subjected to close archaeological examination.

Buşeirah lies 22 kilometres south of Ṭafileh on the King's Highway and then 4 kilometres to the west. The ruins are right at the end of, and at the highest point of, a steady climb through the village and are only joined to the surrounding hills by this neck of land. Thus Buseirah forms a promontory with very steep ravines on three sides. The surrounding wadis converge and eventually find their way to the Wadi Arabah. The plan on the following page (fig. 1a), drawn to a scale of 1:100, shows the site and the areas of excavation. The total area covered by the plan is approximately 81,602 sq. metres. This probably only embraced the most important part of the ancient city, that is, the temple and palace complexes, together with the walled enclosures on the lower terraces for the animals and crops, and for the housing of the servants attached to the royal court and to the temple. Ordinary citizens lived in the area now occupied by the present-day village.

The plan of the excavations was to cut a section right across from the city wall (Area B), through the so-called Acropolis (Area A), through Area D to the east of Area A and on to the eastern defensive city wall. This latter cut never materialised.

For a full discussion of these various areas, and for necessary and relevant notes, reference should be made to the Preliminary Reports in *Levant,* Vols. V, VI, VII, and IX.

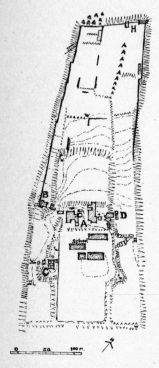

Fig. 1a
Buseirah Site Plan

Fig. 1b
Seal Impression of
Malkibaal
(Not to scale)

The town wall, of a width of 6.8 metres, was probably of
the construction known as casemate, i.e. two parallel walls, not
always of the same thickness, joined at intervals by a transverse
wall. The areas enclosed by these walls could be used either
as store rooms or filled with rubble to strengthen the
fortifications. An earlier wall was found running roughly
parallel to the other two parallel walls. It was impossible
to date this wall with accuracy without removing the later
walls, but judging from the few sherds found, there is no
reason to date the wall earlier than the very end of the 9th
century BC or the early 8th. Against the inner and outer
parallel walls an enormous amount of pottery was found and it
seems clear that on the two occasions that the Acropolis was
sacked, the pottery from Area A (i.e. the Acropolis) was removed
and thrown against the city wall. Typical, small Iron Age II
houses were built against the inner casemate wall and extended up
the slope until they came to a massive barrier wall, which was
probably the dividing line between the aristocracy on Area A
and their servants and dependents on Area B. Area D showed the
same type of houses, though in their latest use these date
probably from the Persian period. Others in Area B had a life
span from the end of the 8th century to the end of the 7th.

An interesting phenomenon at Buseirah, considering its size
and importance, particularly in the neo-Assyrian period, is the
extreme paucity of epigraphical material. One of the more
interesting finds was a seal impression found in a stratified
level outside the gateway in our Area B. (See Fig. 3, *Levant,*
VII, 1975, p. 4). According to the epigraphists, Lemaire (*Levant,*
VII, 1975, pp. 18ff) and Puesch (*Levant,* IX, 1977, pp. 12f), the
seal impression belonged to one Malkibaal, servant of the king
(Fig. 1b). The name corresponds to the well-attested Phoenician
and Punic name *b'lmlk,* which is parallel to the Hebrew names
mlk'l, mlkyh and *mlkyhw.* Whether this seal impression is
Phoenician or Edomite is impossible to decide paleographically.
The Edomite writing by this time (8th-7th cent.) is practically
identical to the Phoenician writing, as is shown by the *ytm* seal
from Tell el Kheleifeh and the inscription on a jug from Umm al
Biyara. The use of the theophoric element *b'l* is already
attested in Edomite names by the seal *lb'zr'l'bdyb'l* from Petra
(see *Levant,* VII, p. 19).

Another interesting phenomenon at Buseirah was the almost
complete lack of luxury goods. What few we had came from the
little houses in Areas B and D. They included a fragment of an

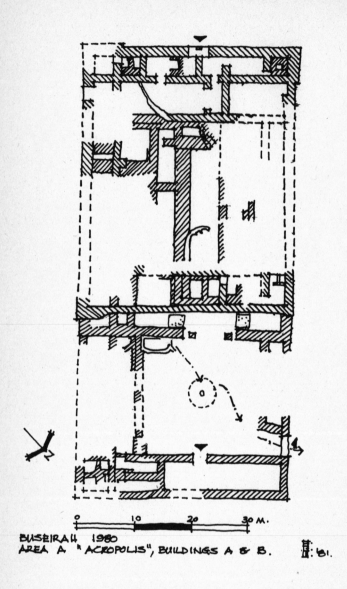

BUSEIRAH 1980
AREA A "ACROPOLIS", BUILDINGS A & B.

Egyptian chalice and a bird of prey engraved on a Tridacna
Squamosa shell. This latter could be of Phoenician,
neo-Assyrian or Cypriot workmanship. The Egyptian chalice
fragment (only 3.1 cms x 2.1 cms) is decorated in relief on
the outside with a plain interior. The glaze with which it
was once coated is now almost completely worn off, leaving
only traces of a blue-green colour. The outer side of the
fragment shows the upper part of a papyrus flower in relief
and above this a hieroglyphic inscription under the rim. The
signs are incuse and are banded with a black painted line.
Three of the signs can be read as *R'dt* and the first two are
probably badly drawn signs for *'nh* and *mi*, the whole group
reading "Given life like Re forever", a common formula appended
to a king's titulary or that of a member of the royal family.
By whatever means the chalice found its way to Buseirah, it
does suggest trade with Egypt. Or it could have been an
heirloom, brought back from Egypt by Prince Hadad who fled
there, according to I Kings 11:14ff. (see J.R. Bartlett, "The
rise and fall of the Kingdom of Edom", *PEQ* 104 (1972), 29ff),
if indeed he returned. But that would have been in the 10th
century BC and no pottery has been found at Buseirah which can
be attributed to so early a date.

Area A, the so-called Acropolis, covering some 2,325 sq.
metres had a very odd, but important feature. The entire area
had a fill varying in depth from 4 to 2 metres into which the
foundations for the earliest buildings were sunk. It was only in
this area that this dark brown earth was found and it seems to
the writer that it was deliberately imported from elsewhere, not
only to support the massive foundations needed for walls standing
some 20 metres high, but to give the Acropolis an overall
dominance over the surrounding countryside. One can image the
effect these buildings would have had on the people passing along
the King's Highway to the south of Buseirah.

In the light of our past excavations we had postulated two
distinct building periods on the Acropolis, which covered some
2,325 sq. m: Building A, the later building, enclosing 1,710 sq.
m. and Building B, the earlier building, some 2,400 sq. m. On
trying to assign walls, particularly in the southern areas of the
building complex B, some of which had been revealed in the 1980
excavations, it became obvious that there must have been an
intermediate period between Buildings A and B (Fig. 2). This
will take intensive study, particularly as there is no depth of
deposit between the building periods. All we have been able to

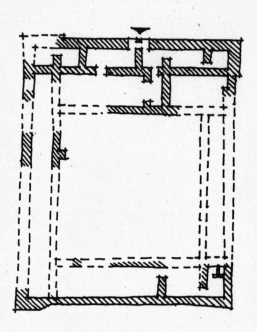

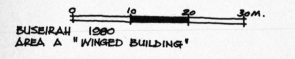

BUSEIRAH   1980
AREA A " WINGED BUILDING"   '81.

do is peel off from Fig. 2 the walls, etc., which we have
reason to believe belong to the "Winged" building, A (Fig. 3).

A brief discussion of buildings A and B might be useful.
In the earliest building B, the outer and inner walls were
covered with a thick plaster, traces of which are visible
throughout the building. Two entrances, both off centre and
near the northern end, were discovered and no doubt similar
entrances would have been found in the southern area under the
"Winged" Building A. The entrances were approached by a ramp,
a feature common to the entrances found in Areas B and C. In
the main central courtyard was a cistern into which water flowed
through two drains: one went diagonally across the main
courtyard and had an outlet through the north-western entrance,
the other emerged from a plastered room, which may have served
as a washing room before entering the holy of holies. At the
end of the courtyard and straddling the north-south axis was a
flight of shallow steps, which had been very badly cracked by
fire and were flanked on either side by two plinths, about
1.20 m. square, on which had rested two wooden columns. The
imprints of their bases can still be seen on the plinths. These
steps led into a long narrow room, which had a hard, white
plaster floor, like all the other floors, including that of
the courtyard.

In this early period, there was a superstructure in mud-
brick over the main gateway in the short eastern wall. This
was destroyed by fire (as was made evident by the burnt bricks),
probably during an attack by the neo-Babylonians. This was the
earliest evidence of a destruction of the site. It seems likely
that the entire building, apart from the open courtyard, had a
mud-brick superstructure, because there was ample evidence of a
re-use of mud-bricks in the western half of the building.

The mud-brick débris was flattened out in the eastern
section of the Acropolis to form a floor for the later, smaller
"Winged" Building. This was built largely on top of the walls
of the earlier building and in general followed its plan, but on
a reduced scale. Again, all the rooms had plastered floors.
This building was also destroyed by fire.

We come then to Area C (see Fig. 1a). This had its
complement on the other side of the present playground, but
unfortunately had been completely bulldozed before we could
stop the work. Area C followed the life cycle of the buildings

on Area A, though no major reconstruction work seems to have
been done between the two major building periods, apart from
minor alterations to some of the rooms. Judging from the
pottery, I think we can admit to a small Persian occupation,
after which the entire site was abandoned save for an
agricultural use of the area by the Romans and much later as
a lucrative source of stone for the local villagers.

From this very broad, but necessarily limited outline, the
reader will have gathered the following. There is no
archaeological evidence to support the story of the king of
Edom refusing passage to Moses, or for a powerful kingdom of
Edom in the time of David and his son Solomon. Biblical
traditions such as Genesis 36:31ff and Numbers 20:14ff
probably reflect 8th-6th century BC conditions. The evidence
for a very impressive occupation and a city with all the
appurtenances of prosperity is overwhelming during the neo-
Assyrian period and is supported by the records in the Assyrian
Annals, and 8th century BC Biblical references to Bozrah
(especially Amos 1:12).

It is evident that this period may be said to have begun
with Tiglath-Pileser III's successful campaigns into Palestine
(734-732 BC), which were the culmination of his policy to control
the economic resources between the Tigris, Euphrates and the
Nile. The states paid tribute, a form of vassalage which had
already been instituted by Adad-Nirari III (810-785 BC) during
his campaigns into Palestine. It should be noted that he did
not destroy, burn or kill, but intimidated and imposed tribute
on the countries in question, which included Edom. Later kings
followed his example.

In the Assyrian Annals, we read of Tiglath-Pileser III
receiving tribute from Bit Sanipu of Bit-Ammon, Salamanu of
Moab and Kaush Malaku of Edom. Tiglath-Pileser's successors,
including Esarhaddon (680-669 BC), exacted more than monetary
tribute: e.g. the subjects of Qos Gabr, king of Edom, Musuri,
king of Moab and Puduil, king of Bit Ammon, together with those
of nineteen other kings, were employed on transporting various
materials to Nineveh for the building of palaces. In
Assurbanipal's reign (668-633 BC), subject peoples were pressed
into military service. Twenty-two kings are listed as helping
him in his wars against Egypt: they included Musuri of Moab,
Amminabdi of Ammon and Qos Gabr of Edom.

Buṣeirah was a very important site for the neo-Assyrians and the reasons for this may well have been strategic and economic. Maybe they wanted an alternative route to Egypt, which would avoid the coastal route, the Via Maris, and by that time the King's Highway was a well established route to Saudi Arabia and countries beyond.

The archaeological evidence also shows the destruction and abandonment of the area of Buseirah in the 6th century BC, no doubt attributable to the Babylonian armies and reflected in such Biblical passages as Isaiah 63:1, Obad. 8 and Jer. 49:13, 22.

(The author would like to thank Dr A.G. Walls for producing at very short notice Figs. 2 and 3, and Miss Sandford for copying Fig. 1).

THE LATE BRONZE AND IRON AGE SITES OF THE WADI EL ḤASĀ SURVEY 1979

Burton MacDonald
Theology Department
St Francis Xavier University
Antigonish
Nova Scotia

The Wadi el Ḥasā Survey 1979 (WHS '79) was in the field from October 28 to December 8, 1979 /1/. The Survey was carried out in a 120 square kilometer area along the south bank of the Wadi el Hasā, Southern Jordan. The Survey territory is bounded on the north by the Wadi el Ḥasā, on the east by the Wadi el La'ban, on the south by the main Ṭafīla-Karak road, and the western boundary is the edge of the plateau where there is a sharp descent to the south-eastern plain of the Dead Sea (Fig. 1). During the in-field season 214 sites were surveyed (Fig. 2). The sites range from lithic and sherd scatters with no architectural remains visible on the surface to very large sites with a great deal of architectural remains visible. Occupation at these sites ranges from prehistoric to modern times or from about 500,000 BC to the end of the Ottoman domination of Jordan in AD 1918 /2/.

This paper will deal with the Late Bronze and Iron Age sites of the Survey only.

Fifteen Middle Bronze-Late Bronze sherds were found at Site 64. A small quantity (4) of what we are reading as Middle Bronze/Late Bronze/Iron Age sherds was found at Site 172.

Late Bronze-Iron I pottery was found at five sites (Sites 106, 145, 147, 168 and 178). In addition Iron IA (1200-1000 BC) sherds were found at four sites (Sites 10, 28, 147 and 212). Moreover, what we are merely reading as Iron I (1200-918 BC) pottery was found at 18 sites (Sites 6, 10, 16, 18, 20, 23, 39, 42, 47, 55, 86, 145, 174, 179, 182, 187, 192 and 212). What we are reading as Iron I-Iron II (1200-539 BC) pottery was found at six sites (Sites 24, 31, 39, 173, 190 and 211). Besides, Iron II (918-539 BC) pottery was found at nine sites (Sites 10, 20, 28, 55, 61, 71, 103, 172 and 187). What we are merely calling Iron Age pottery was found at five sites (Sites 58, 144, 148, 165 and 179) (Fig. 3). There are other sites of the Survey for which the "Field Reading" for the pottery collected is Late Bronze, Iron I, or Iron II possibly, probably and questionably. Further study of these sites is necessary before more definite conclusions can be drawn.

There are more Late Bronze and Iron Age sites in the area than one would have been led to believe on the basis of the work done in the same territory by Nelson Glueck between 1934 and 1940 (*Explorations in Eastern Palestine,* II [*AASOR,* Vol. XV for 1934-35], New Haven, Ct.: American Schools of Oriental Research, 1935, pp. 100-112; *Explorations in Eastern Palestine,* III [*AASOR,* Vols. XVIII-XIX for 1938-39], New Haven, Ct.: American Schools of Oriental Research, 1939, pp. 56-60). A comparison of the findings at the sites common to the WHS '79 and Glueck is instructive (Table 1).

Glueck did not find Late Bronze pottery at any of these 23 common sites. However, we found Late Bronze-Iron I pottery at Ras er-Rḥāb (Site 178) and Kh. 'Ayūn Ghuzlân (Site 145) and possible Late Bronze pottery at Al Gazrain West (Site 144), Kh. Burbeitah (Site 148), and Rabâbeh (Site 172). Glueck found several Edomite EI I-II sherds at Kh. el-Adanîn. We found a great deal of Iron I-IIA (1200-721 BC) pottery at this site (Site 173). Glueck reported Edomite pottery at Kh. es-Sab'ah. This site caused us a great deal of problems insofar as we are not sure that what we are calling Kh. es-Sab'ah (Site 1) is one and the same with the one which Glueck calls by the same name. We collected seven different samples at this site and the predominant pottery in each sample was Byzantine. We found only one possible Iron II sherd at this site. Glueck called Rujm Karaka (Rujm Kerakeh) and Kh. Karaka (Kh. Kerakeh) Edomite fortresses (Glueck 1935: 108-109). We found Iron Age pottery at both these sites (Sites 24 and 31 respectively), but we date it to Iron IC-IIA (1000-721 BC) and thus somewhat later than Glueck (1936: 143; 1970: 153, 161). Glueck found a small number of Edomite sherds at Kh. en-Nôkhah (Glueck 1935: 107). We found both Iron I and Iron II sherds at the site (Site 20). Glueck also found Edomite period pottery at Kh. Baḥlûl and he writes (Glueck 1939: 59): "A small number of EI I-II sherds was also found, showing that the site had been occupied in the Edomite period." We found many sherds at this site (Site 84), but we have identified only three sherds as coming from the Iron Age period and that from Iron II. At other sites common to the WHS '79 and Glueck we found Iron Age pottery at Kh. Bîr Melîh (Site 182), Kh. Bîr Jummah (Site 16), Kh. Mashmîl (Site 23) (cf. also Weippert 1939: 26, 30 and note 57), and Ras er-Rhâb (Site 178) where he does not mention such pottery. We feel that there is a very strong case for Glueck's position that the area south of the Wadi el Hasā was occupied between the 13th-12th and the 8th centuries BC. However, we differ in details as to where that Iron Age occupation was located. We think that Glueck's case could have been strengthened in his own time by a more detailed examination of the sherds at the sites that he did visit.

The results of the first season of work south of Wadi el Hasā indicate that after a period of abandonment the territory was again being settled in the latter part of the Late Bronze Age. There is abundant evidence for occupation throughout the Iron I period. There is, likewise, sufficient evidence to indicate that the area was occupied for most of the Iron II period. However, there is more evidence for the earlier part of the period than for the latter part.

The WHS '81 will be in the field beginning on April 20. For the '81 season work will be concentrated on the Wadi el La'ban and eastward (Fig. 1). The findings of the '81 season will hopefully clarify even more the occupational history of the south bank of the Wadi el Hasā during the Late Bronze-Iron II periods.

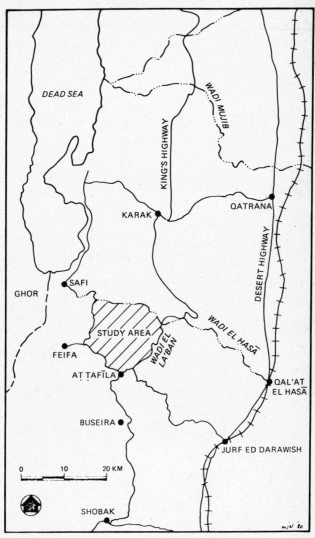

FIGURE 1: Map of Central Jordan with the Survey or
           Study area pinpointed

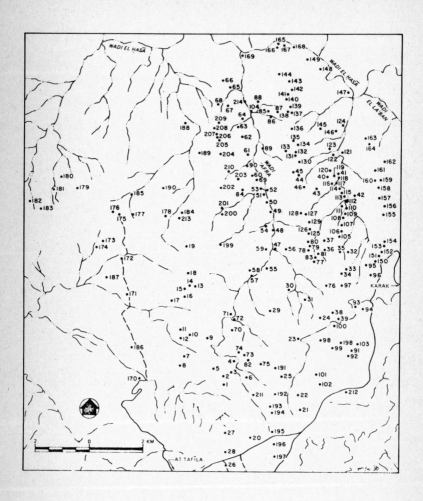

FIGURE 2:   Map of Sites Surveyed

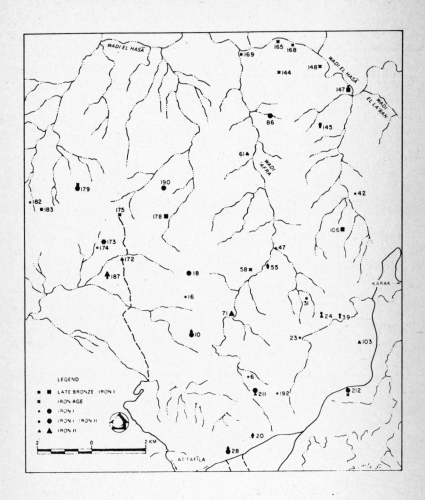

FIGURE 3:   The Late Bronze - Iron II Sites of the WHS '79

Table 1. Comparison of Sites Common to WHS '79 and Glueck

SITE NAME	SITE *:	FIELD READING:
'Aima	170	LIslam-Mod; Byz: Byz; po; LNab-LRom; Mod; PL; Ud sherds and lithics
(el-'Eimeh)*	(206)**	(No sherds collected)**
Dhibâ'a	171	Ott/Mod; Byz: Byz; pr; Nab; Iron Age, po; Ud sherds and lithics
(Ed-Debâ'ah	(207)	(No sherds collected)
Rabâbeh	172	Byz; Nab; Nab, po; Iron II; MB/LB/Iron Age; LB, po; LRom; Ott/Mod: EB IV; Ud sherds and lithics
	(208)	(No sherds collected)
Kh. el-Adanîn	173	Iron I-IIA; LIslam; Byz; EB, po; Ott/Mod, po; MPL; MPL, po; Ud sherds and lithics
	(209)	(Several Edomite EI I-II; few Nab)
Kh. Bîr Melfh	182	Byz; LIslam (Ott); Iron I; Ud; EB backed blade (Some Nab)
	(210)	
Kh. Musrab	177	Byz; Ott/Mod; Nab; Ud; MPL
	(211)	(Few Nab and Mod Arabic)
Kh. Rihâb	184	LIslam; Ott/Mod; Byz; Mod; Ud lithic
	(212)	(No sherds collected)
Gnan el-Qarn)	13	Ayy/Mam; Byz/Mam; Byz; Mod; Ud; MPL
(Kh. el-Qarn)	(213)	(Some Nab and Arabic)

Site	No.	Description
Kh. Bîr Jummah	16	Byz; Iron I; Nab; LRom; Ayy/Mam; Ud
	(214)	(Few Nab and Mod Arabic)
'h. es-Sab'ah	1	Byz; Iron II, po; LIslam; Mod; Byz/Umy, po; Nab; LRom
	(215)	(Some Edomite and Nab)
Kh. Abû Benna	212	Iron IA; Iron I; Iron Age; Byz; LOtt/Mod; Mod; Nab; LIslam; Ud sherds and lithics
(Kh. Abû Benneh	(230)	(Edomite EI I-II; Nab; Rom; Mediaeval Arabic)
Kh. en-Nôkhah	20	Ayy/Mam; Byz; Iron I; Iron II; LRom; Ud
	(231)	(Arabic; Edomite; Nab; Rom)
Kh. Mashmîl	23	Byz; Iron I; Iron I, po; EB IVA; Ayy/Mam; LIslam; LRom; Ud; MPL flakes
	(232)	(Bronze Age, ca.2200-1800 BC; Nab; Rom)
Rujm Karaka	24	Iron IC-IIA; Iron II; LIslam; LRom; LRom; Byz; Ud
(Rujm Kerakeh)	(233)	(Some Edomite)
Kh. Karaka	31	LIslam; Iron IC-IIA; Byz; Mod; Ud sherds and lithics
(Kh. Kerakeh)	(234)	(No sherds collected)
Kh. 'Ayûn Ghuzlân	145	Nab/LRom; Nab; LB-Iron, Ud; Iron I; LIslam; Mod; LPL-MPL; MPL; UD
	(56)	(Nab; Late Arabic [?])
Kh. Bahlûl	84	Nab; LIslam; LRom; Iron II, po; LPL-MPL; Ud
	(57)	(Nab; 'Pergamene' Sigillata; small number of EI I-II)

'Ain De'es North	85	Nab; LRom; Ud; PL
(Kh. Ḥedeis)	(58)	(Nab; wasters and tiles)
Al Gazrain West	144	Nab; Byz; Iron Age; LIslam; LB, po; LRom; Ud; EPL-ENL; PL
('Ain Qasrein)	(59)	(Nab-Rom; Byz; piece of 'Pergamene' sigillata)
Kh. el-Burbeiṭah	148	Byz; Mod; Nab; Iron Age; LB, po; Hell; LIslam; Ud sherds and lithics
	(60)	(Nab; Rom-Byz; Mediaeval Arabic)
Kh. Ḥammâm	149	Nab; Mod; Ud; EPL-ENL; UPL
	(61)	(Nab; piece of 'Pergamene' sigillata)
Kh. es-Sabrah	188	LIslam; Nab; po; Ud sherds and lithics
	(62)	(Mediaeval Arabic; Byz, po)
Ras er-Rhâb	178	Byz; LBIron I; Iron I-II; Ott/Mod; LRom; LIslam; Nab, po; Hell, pr; MPL; UD sherds and lithics
(Kh. er-Rhâb)	(63)	(Nab-Rom; Late Arabic)

* Where the spelling of the site name differs, Glueck's spelling is given in parentheses.

** Glueck's Site Number and Field Reading are given in parentheses. Sites are listed according to the order in which Glueck discovered them. WHS '79 Field Reading lists sherds according to quantity.

NOTES

/1/   Besides the writer who served as project director, the
survey team consisted of Ted Banning, a graduate student in the
Department of Near Eastern Studies in the University of Toronto,
Larry Pavlich, a graduate in the Department of Anthropology of
the same university, and Nabil Begain, representative of the
Department of Antiquities of Jordan. The reading of the flints
and sherds was done by Dr James A. Sauer, Director, American
Center of Oriental Research (ACOR) in Amman. While in the field
the team stayed at a rented house in Ṭafila which is situated just
south of the survey area (Fig. 1). The weekends were spent in
residence at ACOR. The project was financed by a grant from the
Social Sciences and Humanities Research Council of Canada (Grant
Number: 410-78-0533). Financial help for the publication of the
results of the survey was received from the University Council for
Research (CC/61) of St Francis Xavier University. The project was
licenced by the Department of Antiquities of Jordan. It is an
affiliated project of the American Schools of Oriental Research.
Maps for this article were prepared by Mary Jane Westland. A
travel grant to participate in the Colloquium was received from
the Office of International Relations of the Social Sciences and
Humanities Research Council of Canada (Grant Number 461-81 0065).
/2/   An article entitled "The Wadi el Hasā Survey, 1979: A
Preliminary Report," has appeared in the *Annual of the Department
of Antiquities of Jordan,* XXIV (1980); 169-183. Brief reports
on the Survey have appeared in the *Bulletin of the Canadian
Society for Archaeology Abroad* 19 (1980): 19-23; in the "Notes
and News" segment of *Biblical Archaeologist* 44 (1 1981: 60-61)
and in the *American Schools of Oriental Research Newsletter,*
Number 3, December 1980, pp. 5-12. A report on Site 104 of the
survey has appeared in *Liber Annuus* (Studii Biblici Franciscani),
XXX (1980): 351-364, pls. 59-70, under the title "The Hermitage
of John the Abbot at Hammam 'Afrā, Southern Jordan."

References in the Text

Glueck, N.

    1935   *Explorations in Eastern Palestine,* II, *AASOR*
           Vol. XV for 1934-1935. New Haven, Ct.: American
           Schools of Oriental Research

    1936   "The Boundaries of Edom," HUCA 11: 141-157

1939   *Explorations in Eastern Palestine,* III, *AASOR,*
        Vols. XVII-XIX for 1938-1939. New Haven, Ct.:
        American Schools of Oriental Research

1970   *The Other Side of the Jordan.* Revised Edition,
        Cambridge, Ma.: American Schools of Oriental
        Research

Weippert, M.

1979   "The Israelite 'Conquest' and the Evidence from
        Transjordan," in *Symposia Celebrating the
        Seventy-fifth Anniversary of the American Schools
        of Oriental Research (1900-1975).* Vols. 1 and 2.
        Edited by Frank Moore Cross. Cambridge, Ma.:
        American Schools of Oriental Research, pp. 15-34

SOCIAL-RELIGIOUS DISTINCTIONS IN IRON AGE BURIAL PRACTICE IN JORDAN

Khair Yassine
Jordan University
Amman, Jordan

Even though the number of tombs discovered in Jordan of the Iron Age period is still relatively small, it is possible to draw from the available data many conclusions concerning social-religious distinctions in Iron Age burial practice.

Burials can reveal more than the level of technology at a particular time. Careful study of burial practices in a certain area may throw light on social behaviour and religious beliefs, since burial rites tend to be more conservative and less susceptible to outside influence and changing fashion than other remains of ancient peoples. Unless there are repeated and frequent occurrences of certain uniform traits, no absolute rule can be given. But if each case is studied on its own merits, in the light of the total evidence available, the archaeologist can hope to identify social and religious distinctions.

From periods or areas from which little or no written material has survived, religious beliefs and social behaviour must be surmised from material remains: types of tombs, their shapes and plans, have to be studied and analysed. A specific feature might indicate some special trait: for example, secondary burials and the idea behind them, which many have tried to relate to social behaviour.

Possibly the position and orientation of the body might indicate social or religious distinction. Moslems, for instance, are buried with their faces towards Mecca. Beliefs about death and the afterlife can be deduced from the way the bodies are arranged. Gifts placed in the tombs and other burial customs observed by the excavators can indicate social differentiation, as can the lavishness of different tombs, the pyramid, the mastaba, and the pit grave.

29

Tomb types

     In the past decade several Iron Age tombs were discovered
in Jordan, either accidentally or by a well-organized excavation.
Their types range from natural or artificial caves dug into rock
or earth, to shaft tombs, dug in rock or built in soft earth.
Other types comprise those built of mud brick, stone tombs, and
pit graves. Natural caves used for burial were the most common
type during the Iron Age, especially in the mountain area where
many natural caves were in existence; e.g. Madaba Tomb A /1/,
Sahab D /2/, Nebo/el Mukhiat /3/. The people of Iron Age Jordan,
besides using natural caves to bury their dead, used artificial
caves dug in the soft lime rock near the rocky area, not far
from their towns or settlements. It is possible that these
caves were a natural development from the most common type of
tomb in the Bronze Age, that is, the shaft tomb, where the
builder had to dig in soft lime rock. Tombs such as these were
discovered in Irbid A, Band C /4/, Madaba B /5/, Dibbon J1, J2,
J3, J6, J7, J8 /6/, Siran /7/, Adoni Nur in Amman /8/, Jabel
el-Jofeh as-Sharqi /9/, Sahab B and C /10/, Amman D, B, C /11/,
Amman I in the Roman Theatre /12/, Meqablain /13/.

     Throughout the Iron Age communal burials in caves were
customary. The other communal burial was a shaft tomb type.

     The shaft tombs too were either dug in soft rock or in
earth. A number of these were found, such as the one in
Raghadan Royal Palace in Amman /14/, Sahab A /15/, and two were
found in the Tell el Mazar cemetery, shaft I shaft II /16/.

     The third type in the series is the one built of mud brick.
This type was found in Tell es-Saidiyah, probably from the late
Bronze Age /17/, and the tomb of Tell el-Kheleifeh /18/.

     There is another type, the pit grave, which was a pit dug
in the ground, with no attempt to line it with bricks or stones.
If stones were used, they were used only at one side. This type
of tomb was found in Tell es-Saidiyah /19/, and at the recent
excavation of Tell el Mazar cemetery /20/.

     These were the types of tombs. There were no Charnel
Houses, or dolmen-type burials, or Chambers or Loculi or
circular graves, or rectangular shaft tombs, of which types
existed at one time or another in the Bronze Age (Stiebing 1970).
The use of one type or another must follow certain social or

religious practice. Nowadays, the different tomb type used by
different ethnic and religious groups quite evidently follows
their own social or religious burial practice. The Nabataean
tombs are a clear example of this. The continuity of tomb type,
plan, or shape or the discontinuity can be important in
determining whether or not population changes had occurred.

The arrangement of bodies

The entire burial procedure may be reconstructed from the
situation within the burial ground and its vicinity. In the
cave tomb type, the body of the deceased was laid on the floor,
possibly on a reed mat or other material (decomposed). Evidence
of these was found in Sahab D /21/, Nebo /22/, Madaba /23/,
Irbid B /24/, Amman E, F /25/ and Dibon /26/. In some cases a
stone or rock platform received the human body and the funerary
offerings. Each platform seems to have been designed to hold
one or two bodies or more. The bodies were usually placed on
the platform either extended or contracted. It was difficult
to know, since the reporter failed to note this. When new
burials were made in a tomb already containing a platform, the
earlier were simply pushed aside and the platform reused. The
number of platforms in the individual tombs differs; sometimes
the tomb has one platform as in Irbid C /27/, Amman A /28/, or
two platforms, as found in Sahab B and C /29/, or three platforms
as in Meqablain /30/, and Dibon J1 and J3 /31/. In some cases
the body was laid on a fine coat of mud plaster, as found in
Tell el Mazar /32/.

In many cases extra care was taken in handling the body of
the deceased. Aside from the extra care of putting the deceased
on a platform, it was placed either in a clay container (big
jar, clay coffin, box-like ossuary) or in an anthropoid coffin.
Large jars containing the bones of adults were found in the
Raghadan Royal palace tomb in Amman /33/. They were placed in
a shaft tomb. In Tell el Mazar grave 47, an infant was put in
a broken jar /34/. In Sahab tombs C and D the dead were put
in big jars /35/. These jars were not designed specially for
the purpose, since their mouths had been broken in order to be
able to place the deceased. Two of these were found in Jordan,
one from Adoni Nor in Amman /36/, and one from Tell el Mazar,
grave no. 23. The most elaborate clay coffins are those of the
anthropoid coffins which have been found in countries other than
Jordan. They were found in the Raghadan palace tomb in Amman,
five of them in a shaft tomb /37/, and one in Sahab tomb A /38/.

Secondary burial

Some bodies were placed in tombs in a mass of
disarticulated burials indicating nomadic groups, who carried
with them in bags or clay coffins those who died during seasonal
migrations, burying them in tombs only when the tribe returned
to its traditional burial place /39/. It is also possible that,
if the person was killed somewhere far away from his traditional
burial place, what was left of him was carried in a container
(clay coffin) to the traditional burial place, since the bones
of those found were very incomplete. The third possibility is
that the bodies were first exposed at a designated spot until
the flesh had decayed. The bones were then gathered up and
placed in a container (clay coffin, anthropoid coffin, wide
mouthed storage jars, or bags).

More than one body was found in the anthropoid coffin of
Raghadan Royal Palace Tomb in Amman, and since the size of the
anthropoid coffin is not big enough to house more than one
corpse, it is evident that the flesh had already decayed before
the bodies were placed inside the coffin. In Sahab tomb B and
C and graves 23, 43 and 82 of Tell el Mazar only long bones and
skulls were found. Secondary burials may indicate a particular
reverence for the skull. At Tell el Mazar grave 43, bones were
placed in bundles with the skull semi-attached to them. In
grave 28 long bones and the skull were placed in the clay coffin.

Position and Orientation

After the tomb was prepared, the body was placed in the
chamber or in the grave on its back or on its side, in an
extended or contracted (crouching) position, or as a mass of
disarticulated bones. In Tell el Mazar cemetery, there was a
distinct difference between the position of the male and the
female. The majority of male corpses were placed in an extended
position: in graves 1, 2, 4, 6, 7, 9, 11, 14, 15, 17, 20, 21,
24, 28, 33, 35, 37, 39, 44, 49, 51, 52, 56, 57, 58, 59, 60, 63a,
and 65, all were laid on their back in an extended position,
except 17 who was laid on his right side. The females were put
in a crouching position, as in graves 3, 10, 16, 19, 25, 26, 27,
32, 36, 38, 40, 41, 42, 45, 46, 61, 62, 64, 67, 68, 69, 70, 71, 72,
73, 74, 76, 78, 79, 80, 81, and 83. In other graves it was
difficult to know their exact position since they were mostly
disarticulated.

Both males and females were orientated east-west, heads to the east with few exceptions. Similar to Tell el Mazar were the Tell el Hesi graves /40/ and Tell el 'Ajjul /41/. In those of the MBI period, however, from other places, there seems to have been no consistent attempt to orientate the bodies in one direction.

Beliefs about death and the afterlife

Inferences concerning beliefs about death and the afterlife can be drawn from the ways the bodies were handled, the gifts placed in the tombs, and other burial customs evidenced by the excavations. The placing of pottery vessels in the tomb, for example, may have held liquids or foods to be used in the afterlife, and the presence of expensive and luxury copper objects might also be significant.

There is no suggestion of any deity who would help them to enjoy the afterlife, or protect them in their passage to it.

However, the shaft tomb of the 8th century BC of Tell el Mazar was situated in the room of a shrine and its courtyard. Shaft tomb II was dug in the ground floor of a room (R1 A/C5), while shaft tomb I was dug in the courtyard of the shrine (AE6). The courtyard had a 50 cm ash deposit mixed with pottery sherds and animal bones. A religious procession of some kind must have taken place in the holy courtyard.

Social differentiation

There is evidence that there were great differences in wealth between groups of population. These differences probably reflect social and political differentiations as well. Burial objects like alabaster, bone inlay, silver and copper objects, weapons, like those found in Tell al Mazar and other cemeteries, indicate the wealth of their owners.

Fatality Statistics

From the study of human skeletal remains at Tell el Mazar done by Dr Disi and Dr Kanda /42/, one can deduce that the probability of death was high in the first phase of life, and decreased to zero in the 10-14 year age group. Then we have an increase in the 25-29 year group, a small decline in the late adult phase, and a steady increase in the oldest phase.

Life expectancy among the Tell el Mazar population was
33.48 years, that is about one half of the life expectancy in
modern industrialized populations.

In conclusion, we can say that the derived data fit very
well into the theory that the prehistoric populations existed
in conditions which are comparable with those in undeveloped
countries, with a high mortality rate in young groups and early
adults due to traumatic diseases in males and death in
association with child-birth in females.

Palaeopathology

One of the most interesting observations on the skeletons
from Tell el Mazar was the cranial and post-cranial trepanning.
While trephinning of the vault is well known from different
places all over the world and has been undertaken since the
Stone Age, post-cranial trephinning is very rare. In the
present case the holes are very small (about 4-5 mm in diameter),
but this is in no way an exception. In Mazar the trephine holes
are on the right cranial vault of the skeleton of burial 22 which
has 12 holes. One has only 4 holes. In another case there are
3 holes. When one asks for the motives for undertaking this
operation, we can only guess. In the present case we are of the
opinion that the holes were made shortly before death, or after
death, since no healing process can be observed. We do not know
whether there are medical motives for this procedure, or ritual.
Scepticism that these holes were not necessarily man-made or
have randomly developed can be destroyed by the fact that an
instrument (114.2 mm long and 3.54 to 3.3 mm in diameter) was
found during excavation, which had probably served as a drill
for trepanning the demonstrated holes /43/.

NOTES

/1/   Harding, G.L., "An Early Iron Age Tomb at Madaba",
Palestine Exploration Fund Annual 6 (1957), pp. 27-47.
/2/   Ibrahim, M., "Third Season of Excavations at Sahab, 1973",
Annual of Jordan, 20.
/3/   Saller, S. "Iron Age Tombs at Nebo, Jordan", *Liber Annuus
Studii Biblici Franciscani* 16 (1969), pp. 165-298.
/4/   Dajani, R.W.,"Four Iron Age Tombs from Irbid", *ADAJ* 2
(1966), p. 88.

/5/   Piccirillo, M., "Una Tomba del Ferro I A Madaba (Madaba B-Moab)", *Liber Annuus Studii Biblici Franciscani* 25 (1975), pp. 199-224.

/6/   Tushingham, A.D., "The Excavations at Dibon (Dhiban) in Moab. The Third Campaign in 1952-53", *Annual of the American Schools of Oriental Research* 40 (1972), p. 89.

/7/   Ibrahim, M., "Archaeological Excavations in Jordan, 1972", *ADAJ* 7 (1972), pp. 93-95.

/8/   Harding, L., "The Tomb of Adoni Nur in Amman", *PEFQ* 6 (1953), pp. 27-47.

/9/   Dajani, R., "An Iron Age Tomb from Amman (Jabel el Sharqi)", *ADAJ* 2 (1966), pp. 48-52.

/10/   Dajani, R. "A Late Bronze-Iron Age Tomb Excavated at Sahab, 1968", *ADAJ* 5 (1970), pp. 29-34.

/11/   Harding, L., "Two Iron Age Tombs at Amman", *QDAP* 11 (1945), pp. 47-74.

/12/   Harding, L., "Two Iron Age Tombs at Amman", *ADAJ* 6 (1971), pp. 37-40.

/13/   Dornemann, R., *The Cultural and Archaeological History of Transjordan in the Bronze Ages,* Chicago, 1970, pp. 460-462.

/14/   Yassine, K., "Anthropoid Coffins from Raghadan Royal Palace Tomb in Amman", *ADAJ* 10 (1975), pp. 75-86.

/15/   Albright, W., "An anthropoid clay coffin at Sahab, Transjordan", *American Journal of Archaeology* 36 (1932), pp. 295-306.

/16/   Yassine, K., *The Cemetery of Tell el Mazar, Jordan* (forthcoming).

/17/   Pritchard, J., *The Cemetery of Tell es-Saidiyah, Jordan,* Philadelphia, University of Pennsylvania, 1980.

/18/   Glueck, N., "The Third Season of Excavations at Tell el Kheleifeh", *BASOR* 79 (1940), pp. 2-18.

/19/   Supra 17.

/20/   Supra 16.

/21/   Supra 2, p. 31.

/22/   Supra 3, p. 167.

/23/   Supra 1, pp. 27ff.

/24/   Supra 4, pp. 88ff.

/25/   Supra 11, pp. 48ff.

/26/   Supra 6, pp. 89ff.

/27/   Supra 4, p. 88.

/28/   Supra 11, p. 67.

/29/   Supra 2, p. 94.

/30/   Supra 14, pp. 48ff.

/31/   Winnett, F. and Reed, W., "The Excavations at Dibon (Diban) in Moab. Part I: The First Campaign 1950-51. Part II: The Second Campaign 1952", *AASOR* 36-37 (1957-58), pp. 57ff.

/32/   Supra 16.
/33/   Supra 14.
/34/   Supra 16.
/35/   Supra 10, p. 31.
/36/   Supra 8, p. 6.
/37/   Supra 14, pp. 85ff.
/38/   Supra 15, p. 301.
/39/   Kenyon, K. *Jericho I,* 1965, p. 59.
/40/   Coogan, M.D., "A Cemetery from the Persian Period at
Tell el Ḥesi", *BASOR* 220 (1975), pp. 39-46.
/41/   Petrie, W.F., *Ancient Gaza II* (1932).
/42/   Didi, Kenda, Whale, *The Human Skeletal Remains of Tell
el Mazar* (forthcoming).
/43/   *Ibid.*

PAINTED POTTERY OF TAYMA AND PROBLEMS OF CULTURAL CHRONOLOGY IN NORTHWEST ARABIA

Garth Bawden
Peabody Museum
Harvard University
Cambridge, Massachusetts   02138
U.S.A.

Introduction

       This paper examines Midianite pottery in its original cultural context - the settlement. A peculiarly Saudi Arabian viewpoint is utilized, all the data used in the study being derived from sites located in the Northern Hejaz and adjacent areas. The data were collected during several seasons of archaeological work sponsored and supervised by the Saudi Arabian Department of Antiquities and Museums as part of its comprehensive survey of the country. Acknowledgements and thanks are due to the Department and its director, Dr Abdullah Masry, for the opportunity granted the author to participate in this valuable project.

       Although the chief purpose of the comprehensive survey as applied to the northwestern region of Saudi Arabia was to locate and preliminarily date sites, the author had the good fortune to spend the greater part of two field seasons conducting excavations in several significant and well-known sites in danger of being destroyed by proposed agricultural and commercial development. Thus the important oases of Al 'Ula and Tayma each provided the focus for several weeks of intensive survey with associated excavation. The results of these projects supplemented by earlier and continuing general surveys in the region, particularly that conducted at the site of Qurayyah, produced the information on which this paper is based. Archaeological investigation at the large settlement of Tayma proved especially important for adding to existing understanding of the Midianite pottery style, providing as it did clear-cut surface, architectural and stratigraphic contexts for the associated ceramic materials.

It is clear that conclusions based on the type of
preliminary investigations discussed in this study must be
regarded as tentative. However, the foundations of these
conclusions in controlled archaeological procedures elevates
them from the level of superficial surmise to that of
scientifically-derived hypothesis. Such hypothesis constitutes
a set of problems concerning Midianite pottery which will help
direct the future course of study in the northwestern region of
Saudi Arabia along worthwhile and productive pathways.

Present knowledge of Midianite pottery in the northwest of
Saudi Arabia rests largely on the results of the 1968 survey
sponsored by the University of London Institute of Archaeology
(Parr, Harding, Dayton 1970). This expedition visited the
large ancient settlement of Qurayyah 70 kilometres northwest
of Tebuk, performed mapping of the site and conducted a
valuable analysis of its ceramic component. The study concluded
that Qurayyah is overwhelmingly associated with the Midianite
pottery style. This style as defined at the site by a large
surface collection incorporates several distinctive decorative
and structural traits. Paste ranges in colour from cream to red,
the majority of pieces containing coarse temper; most vessels
are wheel-made with common shapes being bowls and platters with
sigmoid rim profiles. The most characteristic decorative scheme
incorporates polychrome patterns of red, black, yellow and
brown on cream slip. However some bichrome painting is also
used. Designs are often naturalistic in inspiration, birds and
animals constituting common themes while geometric features also
occur (Parr, Harding, Dayton 1970:238).

This description, as defined at Qurayyah, at present
remains the definitive stylistic denominator of Midianite
pottery in Saudi Arabia with additional survey, while revealing
hitherto undetected modifications, essentially confirming its
conclusions and somewhat widening its known distribution to
Tayma, approximately 260 kilometres to the southeast (Winnett
and Reed 1970; Bawden, Edens and Miller 1980) and several other
sites in the northern coastal portion of the Hejaz (Michael
J. Ingraham: personal communication). It thus appears on the
basis of presently available evidence that the Saudi Arabian
distribution of Midianite pottery and its related culture
extends northward from a point somewhat north of the Al 'Ula
oasis to the Jordanian frontier and reaches at least as far
east as Tayma, encompassing the entire northwestern corner of
the Arabian peninsula.

Midianite Pottery: Distribution and Style

Beyond the northwestern frontier of Saudi Arabia, Midianite pottery is chiefly known through the work of Beno Rothenberg at Timna where a sample of the style displays the same decorative and structural characteristics as that described for Qurayyah (Rothenberg 1972). However, a small quantity of Midianite pottery has also been identified at the site of Kheleifeh in the southern Arabah (Glueck 1967), various eastern Arabah sites (Glueck 1935) and the island of Jazirat Fara'un south of Elat (Rothenberg 1972:204). Further isolated finds have occurred at the southern end of the Dead Sea, on the Mediterranean coast of the Sinai, near Petra and elsewhere in the region (Parr 1970:239). Thus the northern presence of Midianite pottery seems confined to the areas of the Arabah, Negev and Sinai contiguous with its previously described Saudi Arabian distribution. Together these areas constitute a homogeneous ceramic region which is clearly defined both in terms of its borders and internal consistency.

The consistency seen in the distribution of Midianite pottery does not extend to its occurrence frequency. A brief survey of proportional occurrence in those sites which contain the style immediately reveals a differential presence. At the two southern sites that have been adequately studied - Qurayyah and Tayma (Parr 1970; Bawden et al. 1980), Midianite pottery clearly comprises a major component of the ceramic corpus present. This situation contrasts vividly with the pattern north of Qurayyah where except at the Hathor Temple of Timna, where Midianite wares constituted 25% of the pottery recovered, only very small lots of this type occur north of the Saudi Arabian frontier. In addition it has been noted by Rothenberg (1972:163) that the paste and temper of Midianite pottery found at Timna is atypical of the region. However these structural characteristics in general conform to those observed by Parr at Qurayyah and the author at Tayma. These features of occurrence frequency and structural affinity strongly support the suggestion of Parr (1970:24) and Rothenberg (1972:182f) that the homeland of the makers of Midianite pottery was in the northern Hejaz.

It is generally accepted at present that Midianite pottery dates to the Late Bronze Age. Although Glueck (1967:20), basing his analysis on comparative data from the Arabah and Edomite sites of the region, proposes a date falling between the late 8th and 6th centuries BC, most scholars argue for an earlier

chronology. Parr (1970:238f) distinguishes between Glueck's
Edomite ware and Midianite pottery and tends toward a date in
the final centuries of the 2nd millennium BC for the latter.
At Timna Rothenberg found a large quantity of Midianite ware in
apparently firm archaeological association with an Egyptian
temple dating to the XIX and XX Dynasties, hence no later than
the 12th century BC (Rothenberg 1972:280ff). Thus the prevailing
current view sees Midianite pottery and culture as dating
predominantly to the Late Bronze Age. It is, however, important
to note that Rothenberg has raised the possibility of the Timna
and Qurayyah wares representing part of a larger ceramic
tradition (1972:182). This suggestion is especially pertinent
given the so far superficial nature of Midianite pottery
analysis in its Hejaz "hearthland" and the presence in the
region of other painted pottery styles with generally similar
decorative motifs and dates which span the 1st millennium BC.
These styles include Midianite pottery itself, and the later
mid-1st millennium styles seen at Khuraibah and also appears
in the Al 'Ula oasis (Parr 1970:204ff; Bawden 1979). Thus the
actual formal and chronological boundaries of the Midianite
wares remain somewhat undefined, involving questions regarding
the exact decorative and structural parameters of the Timna and
Qurayyah Midianite ceramic components and their chronological
and geographic relationships. The recent work at the site of
Tayma helps to clarify these parameters and pose further
problems relative to the pottery and its cultural implications.

Tayma: Description and History

     The oasis of Tayma is located roughly 150 kilometres
northeast of Al 'Ula and 220 kilometres southeast of Tebuk,
lying on the main Tebuk-Medina road. The modern town of Tayma
is the present-day manifestation of long-lasting settlement at
the oasis. Tayma is mentioned in Assyrian, Neo-Babylonian and
Biblical texts as an important settlement and also appears
frequently in Islamic records. Moreover, a Nabatean presence
is reflected architecturally at the site. (See Bawden et al.
1980:71-74 for full bibliographic record). The primary
importance of Tayma to the general pre-Islamic period and more
specifically to the temporal focus of this study - the Late
Bronze and Iron Ages - undoubtedly lay in its strategic location
at the hub of a communications network which connected southern
Arabia with Egypt, Syria and Mesopotamia. It is apparent from
the texts that this situation intermittently brought Tayma and
its northern Arabian counterparts, Dawmat-al-Jandal and Dedan,

into direct contact with the expansionist states to the north.
Thus Assyrian texts written during the reign of Tiglath-Pileser
III (744-727 BC) mention the exaction of tribute from eight
northern Arabian cities and tribes including Tayma from which
spice was exacted in tribute. Subsequent Assyrian rules
attempted to maintain this dominance of north Arabia.

The most dramatic recorded involvement of Tayma with a
foreign power occurred soon after 555 BC when the last
Neo-Babylonian king, Nabonidus, conquered the town and resided
there for ten years. The reasons for this extraordinary event
which made Tayma *de facto* capital of the Neo-Babylonian empire
are yet to be satisfactorily explained but are probably due to
a combination of factors. Such factors include Nabonidus'
conflict with the priests of Babylon due to his elevation of the
moon god Sin of Harran over the principal god of the Babylonian
pantheon, Marduk, a possible desire to create a commercial
empire in Arabia controlled through domination of the trade
routes and need to build a new power center from which to combat
the growing power of Persia. According to the texts Nabonidus
built a palace during his sojourn, embellished the town and
constructed perimeter walls, converting Tayma into a fitting
seat for a powerful monarch and his retinue. This textual
indication of extensive architectural construction is extremely
significant when viewed in association with the archaeological
survey conducted by the author at the site.

It can validly be assumed that northern Arabian centres of
the importance of Tayma not only passed through periods of
foreign domination during pre-Islamic times but also experienced
long periods of autonomy during which they themselves flourished
by controlling the long-distance trade routes. Indeed Biblical
mention of the lands of Midian and Edom suggest that at times
these local polities were influential politically as well as
economically in the affairs of the general region. Thus the
archaeological record at Tayma may be expected to reflect the
fluctuating political and commercial relationships of this
strategic location, with local development being intermittently
interrupted and modified by strong foreign intrusion. The
Tayma archaeological survey clearly identified such a pattern
and in so doing poses important questions regarding the nature
of Midianite and subsequent occupation of the town.

The ancient town of Tayma, bounded on three sides by
stone-built perimeter walls and open to the north, covers an

area of roughly 6 km^2. Standing centrally within this area is
the modern town, over 2 km^2 in area, surrounded by cultivated
gardens. Between the periphery of the modern town and the
ancient walls lies a large area of relatively undisturbed
ground containing several extensive concentrations of ancient
stone architecture, including walled enclosures and room
complexes. Cemeteries are located outside of the ancient town
to the south and east while ancient field systems are evident
in the level *sabkha* to the north. Beyond the *sabkha,* a line
of small stone towers and walled compounds line the Riba Hills
which command the northern approaches to the town.

The Tayma archaeological survey of 1979 included two
major strategical components. First, intensive surface survey
attempted to identify and map all occupational loci associated
with the pre-Islamic town. Second, limited test excavations
were conducted throughout the area in order to define the nature
of such occupation, determine its chronological identity and if
possible to recover data which could shed light on wider
temporal and spatial relationships. Although, because of the
small amount of time available and the great size of the site,
aims were of necessity limited, important information was
recovered pertaining to aspects of occupational depth,
settlement organization and cultural development. The two chief
sources of this data - ceramic and architectural material -
offered sufficient information to allow the construction of a
general framework for the history of Tayma.

Tayma: Ceramics

As a result of the 1979 survey several distinct ceramic
styles were revealed at Tayma. Various of these styles could
readily be defined by comparison to those already well known
through work elsewhere in the general region of northwest
Arabia and southern Jordan. Others still await proper
identification. The familiar styles include a large body of
painted wares which relate closely to Midianite pottery as
known through the Qurayyah survey and Timna excavations and
small quantities of Khuraibah and Nabatean pottery. Other wares
represented at Tayma include examples which generally relate to
the rather vaguely defined Hellenistic ceramic styles seen
elsewhere in northern Arabia, and wares confined to cemetery
contexts and having few or no known regional affines (see Bawden
et al. 1980 for full ceramic analysis).

The painted wares found at Tayma constitute by far the
largest decorated ceramic component in the ancient town.
However, several decorative classes appear to be represented
within this general painted category. A prominent class is
comprised of fragments which both in terms of construction and
decoration are identical to Midianite pottery as it has been
previously described. Paste is generally of the light red and
light brown colour values with variable quantities of mostly
dark temper. The decorative scheme utilizes polychrome colour
with red, black, brown and yellow painted over cream or buff
slip. Similarly the range of design motifs associated with this
polychrome pottery exactly corresponds to that which
characterizes Midianite pottery elsewhere. Rather elaborate
use of free-flowing line in abstract and well-executed
curvilinear design dominates the decorative scheme, with
examples of naturalistic forms also being represented. It
should be noted that purely geometric design with angular form
comprises a minor constituent in this scheme. This class of
polychrome painted pottery equates precisely with Midianite
wares collected by Parr at Qurayyah and those from Timna
published by Rothenberg. Thus, it appears clear that there
is a major Midianite ceramic component at Tayma and that the
town may safely be regarded as an important addition to the
known assemblage of Midianite occupation sites.

Important though this characteristic Midianite pottery
component is for furthering understanding of wider ceramic and
cultural relationships of the region, it constitutes a minority
class at Tayma. A much larger category of painted pottery is
decorated with a dark brown to black on cream or buff bichrome
scheme. Most of this pottery contains light red to cream paste
with medium to small amounts of temper, of variable composition
and colour. In these structural aspects the bichrome pottery is
generally similar to the polychrome Midianite material. Moreover,
the most frequent shapes - plates and bowls - are common to both
ceramic classes. However, embellishment clearly differs. The
curvilinear elements, flowing line and complex motifs of
Midianite pottery are largely absent from the bichrome ceramics.
Instead, simple angular geometric designs dominate the decorative
scheme with cross-hatching and bands of vertical lines prevailing.
In addition the careful execution that typifies Midianite
polychrome pottery is replaced by less consistency of colour
and precision of line. Slip colour ranges from cream to buff,
the latter colours often appearing with simple, poorly drawn
motifs in which the strong contrast which characterizes most of

Tayma painted pottery is largely absent. Thus the Tayma
bichrome wares themselves encompass a wide stylistic range with
considerable variation existing in decorative quality, formal
design, and colour value. This variation is significant to the
interpretative thesis suggested in the present study.

Tayma: Architectural Remains

         The architecture of Tayma may best, for the purposes of
this study, be divided into two categories. The first category
is comprised of the massive perimeter walls which mark the
boundaries of the ancient town and in the south enclose a
series of large enclosures. These walls are well preserved
although partially buried by windblown sand in many places;
they are uniformly constructed from sandstone blocks, double-
faced with cores of rubble fill. Several formal gateways
occur in the perimeter walls; these are now largely preserved
as simple openings although excavation suggested that some may
originally have possessed more elaborate flanking features.
The perimeter walls are continuous on three sides of Tayma. To
the north, with the exception of a much lower and less sturdy
wall, the town lies open. Here an extensive expanse of level
sabkha fills the area between the town and the Riba Hill range
approximately two kilometres distant. Vestiges of ancient
agriculture including field systems and irrigation ditches
extend across the *sabkha*; however, association of this
agricultural activity with the pre-Islamic period has yet to
be confirmed.

         The second category of architectural remains consists of
several concentrations of roomed architecture. The largest
such concentration is located in the enclosure complex at the
southern extremity of the ancient town. At this location an
architectural mound has been formed from the superimposed
residue of several periods of building activity. At present
the uppermost of these building strata is represented by a
massive stone-walled structure, known locally as the Qasr Ablaq,
probably abandoned since the first centuries AD and associated
with Nabatean and Lihyanite artefacts. Beneath this structure
is clear ceramic evidence of occupation extending at least into
the Iron Age. A second important architectural complex, the
Qasr Radim, is located about half-way along the western
perimeter wall. This structure, built on superficial bedrock,
is constructed from large stone blocks, is rectangular in shape
and built around a well, now dry. The original structure has

undergone considerable alteration during the Islamic period
with a camel draw replacing one entire side and interior
partition walls also being added. While the latest use of the
Qasr Radim extends well into the Islamic period, the original
structure dates at least to the Iron Age.

The third architectural complex, and one of extreme
importance for understanding the cultural development of Tayma,
stands on a ridge which marks the termination of the western
perimeter wall. The preserved remains of this complex - the
Qasr Al Hamra - include three distinct concentrations of walls
and terraces scattered along the summit of the ridge. The two
southern components consist of rectangular rooms enclosed by
massive stone walls; the third is a series of terraces and small
rooms located at the northern end of the ridge overlooking the
sabkha. It is this small architectural complex which provides
one of the most valuable bodies of data yet recovered from
northwest Arabia.

Limited clearing of this complex reveals that the end of
the ridge has been terraced and is surmounted by a small
platform, open to the north and backed by small walled chambers.
Construction is of the finest quality, with shaped red and grey
sandstone slabs forming the floors and walls of the complex.
Standing directly on the platform floor in a formal pattern
which suggested that they remained in their original
configuration were a number of objects obviously of specialized
function. Present were a stone cube, carved in low relief on
two faces, and several low stone tables, one of which carried
a number of small carefully fashioned stone objects. Several
small fire-blackened bowls and a fragment from an alabaster
vessel also stood on the platform, while the adjoining chamber
was scattered with charcoal and burnt goat and sheep bone. In
addition a large broken stela lay in the fill just above floor
level; evidently this object had been removed from its original
location. The character of this assemblage and its architectural
context strongly indicate that the Qasr Al Hamra represents a
formal religious setting still containing its related ritual
paraphernalia.

The most important individual feature from the platform,
in terms of cultural relationship, is the stone cube. This
object carries relief decoration, Mesopotamian in general
character, on two faces (see Atlal, Vol. 3, Plate 49, 1979 and
Atlal, Vol. 4, Plate 69, 1980). One face bears the

representation of an individual approaching a stepped altar over
which is carved a frontal bull head with a disc between its
horns. Also portrayed are the winged-disc motif commonly
associated with the dominant divinity of the Babylonian religious
pantheon Marduk, a crescent representing the moon-god and a rayed
star, the Venus symbol of the goddess Ishtar. These symbols
also appear on the second carved face where they accompany an
individual who is apparently making an offering to a pacing
bull, also with a disc between its horns.

     The dominant iconographic character of this decorative
scheme is Mesopotamian in its content and execution. The
majority of the motifs present occur in the Mesopotamian
artistic tradition, most of them including the symbols for
divinities and the general offertory theme being very common.
Moreover, in the general softness of execution and specific
features, such as the pacing bull whose stance closely resembles
forms on the Ishtar Gate at Babylon, the work appears southern
in character, approximating Babylonian rather than Assyrian
work. By contrast the frontal bull head is extremely uncommon
in Mesopotamian art; however it commonly appears in the religious
art of the South Arabian states where it invariably represents
the moon god, the principal deity of the region. Thus the
various expressions of the South Arabian moon-god - Kumguh of
Saba, 'Amm of Qataban, Wadd of Ma'in and Sin of Hadramaut, are
all symbolized by a bull, whether in stone sculpture or metal
coinage. Usually the frontal head occurs but occasionally and
especially on coins a standing form is used.

     In addition to this marked South Arabian component the
Tayma sculpture also incorporates an element which can be traced
originally to Egypt. The disc which appears between the bull's
horns in both representations bears a close link to the cow
motif of the goddess Hathor which has a long iconographic
tradition in Egypt prior to the Arabian forms. Thus it appears
likely that several cultural expressions are represented here.
A Mesopotamian presence, probably late Babylonian, is dominant
but is clearly accompanied by an indigenous Arabian element which
in turn has been influenced by earlier Egyptian contact.

     The stela found in the fill directly above the platform
floor also suggests cultural blending. The carved face of the
object contains divinity motifs identical to those on the cube.
These motifs surmount an Aramaic dedicatory inscription of the
mid-1st millennium BC of southern Mesopotamian type (see *Atlal*,

Vol. 3, Plate 49, 1979). This stela thus parallels in form and content the inscription from the famous "Tayma Stone", previously the strongest item of evidence for Mesopotamian presence at Tayma.

Explanation of the Mesopotamian presence rests in historical records. Neo-Babylonian texts attest to the residence of King Nabonidus at Tayma during the 550's and 540's. The appearance on the carved cube of both Mesopotamian and Arabian symbols of the moon god may well reflect the recorded elevation by Nabonidus of the moon god Sin of Harran to a level of unprecedented importance, possibly one of his reasons for leaving Babylon. The Tayma religious expression appears to incorporate native Arabian features into this dominant foreign presence, raising intriguing questions regarding the nature of this cultural syncretism in the 1st millennium BC and the precise relationship of the Tayma sculpture to the Neo-Babylonian occupation.

While confirmation of Neo-Babylonian presence in itself adds greatly to understanding of the site's cultural relationships, the material residue of this presence also raises additional problems pertaining to broader chronological developments at Tayma. The Neo-Babylonian texts clearly state that during the occupation of Tayma Nabonidus built perimeter walls at the town in addition to erecting a palace. This textual evidence would of course date the walls and associated artefacts to the terminal Iron Age in the mid-6th century BC. Examination of the architectural remains in association with surface and stratigraphic survey and Mesopotamian texts indicates that current understanding of the ceramic chronological parameters of much of the Iron Age in the northern Hejaz is incomplete and poses specific problems for future study.

Chronological Implications

In terms of the time period under consideration in the present study - the Late Bronze Age and Iron Age Tayma conforms in its initial and terminal chronological occupational parameters to the pattern noted elsewhere in the region. Those wares which can undeniably be identified with the Midianite ceramics of Timna and Qurayyah in terms of style represent the oldest definable occupation, presumably dating to the Late Bronze Age. Similarly Tayma parallels its more northerly counterparts in its terminal occupational component, Nabatean wares heralding the

appearance of Hellenistic culture at the end of the lst
millennium BC. However, unlike Timna and Qurayyah where no
significant occupation has been noted for the intervening
millennium, there is clear evidence of continuity at Tayma.

    Occupation at Tayma during the Iron Age is indicated by
a variety of sources. As previously noted Assyrian texts from
the reign of Tiglath-Pileser III (744-727 BC) record the
subjugation of the town and imposition of tribute which
included spice. This text suggests first that Tayma was an
important centre of Arabian resistance to Assyrian expansion,
and second that it was already prominent in long-distance
trading activities, spice originating in South Arabia. In
order to acquire this valued commodity Tayma must already at
this time have been an important link in the caravan trading
complex. It follows that a significant occupation during the
8th century must be inferred from this information. Further
references in the texts to campaigns of later Assyrian kings
in northern Arabia imply continuing interaction with the
settlements of this region.

    The second firmly defined Iron Age occupation phase at
Tayma has already been discussed. Abundant textual and
archaeological evidence indicate Neo-Babylonian presence in
the town during the mid-6th century BC. As already noted,
textual information asserts that this occupation was associated
with important constructional activity including erection or
extension of the perimeter walls.

    Finally, a small ceramic component relates to the
characteristic pottery style of the site of Khuraibah in the
Al 'Ula oasis a short distance to the southwest. This ceramic
relationship is accompanied by the appearance in both sites of
full-sized human sculpture of identical style, tentatively
identified with the Lihyanite culture dominant at Khuraibah
during the centuries immediately preceding the Hellenistic
expansion into the area. It appears that occupation dating to
this period and of related cultural character was also present
at Tayma.

    It thus seems clear that the thousand year occupational
hiatus observed in the archaeological record at such sites as
Timna and Qurayyah did not occur at Tayma. While there is as
yet no firm evidence for occupation during the early portion
of the Iron Age until the reign of Tiglath-Pileser III in the

mid-8th century - a period of roughly 300 years - it seems
feasible given the obvious importance of the site by this time
that occupation was present earlier, possibly continuous with
the Late Bronze Age Midianite settlement. Moreover, it now
appears most probable that Tayma was occupied continuously from
the time of its earliest textual mention. However, such an
occupational history is utterly unrepresented in the ceramic
record *as it is presently understood*.

    Midianite pottery of the type described by Parr and
Rothenberg does appear at Tayma. However, vessels bearing the
characteristic polychrome painting, curvilinear and naturalistic
motifs and complex decorative scheme of Qurayyah and Timna
pottery constitute only a small portion of the total corpus.
Moreover, this ceramic component has a very intermittent and
sparse surface distribution, displaying no discernible
relationship to standing architectural features.
Stratigraphically fragments have been recovered from deep
layers of the architectural mound standing at the southern
extremity of the site, indicating that they represent an early
constructional phase at this location. Otherwise no
architectural affine has been found.

    By contrast, bichrome pottery possesses a much wider
distribution and appears in much greater quantities. As noted
earlier in the study, bichrome ceramics are generally painted
with much simpler, angular decoration than is Midianite
polychrome and have a distribution which conforms to the
overall area of the ancient town marked by the perimeter walls.
In addition these wares occur in the small structures which
line the Riba Hills north of Tayma. There appears to be little
mixing of bichrome painted wares with other types except in
localized areas, suggesting that later occupation at the
settlement was more constricted in area. Thus bichrome pottery
in general appears to denote the episode of greatest areal
expansion in the occupational history of Tayma.

    It would be tempting to dismiss the bichrome painted
wares of Tayma as merely a regional variant of Midianite pottery
were it not for two occupational circumstances. First, important
occupation at the site dates at least to the mid-8th century but
provides no recognized ceramic or architectural residue. Second,
and much more significant, are the implications of the
Neo-Babylonian textual record. The town walls are described
as being built during Nabonidus' stay at Tayma. It follows that

occupational refuse including pottery should conform in surface
distribution to the settlement area during this period as
defined by the perimeter walls. It is the bichrome ceramic
component which in fact follows this pattern. Hence the
possibility must be admitted pending future confirmation that
a large proportion of the painted bichrome wares at Tayma date
to the mid-1st millennium BC when the size of the town was at
its greatest during and immediately following the Neo-Babylonian
occupation. However, it must be admitted that this interpretation
may well prove simplistic because the bichrome wares contain a
wide range of decorative and structural variation, making it
impossible at this juncture to posit any phase of stylistic or
chronological homogeneity. Indeed it is demonstrable that a
quantity of this material dates even later - to the Lihyanite
period as defined at Khuraibah - a late 1st millennium
expression. This distinctive ware, of relatively poor quality,
simple decorative content and non-contrasting paint and slip
colour, makes up only a minor component of the total bichrome
corpus but does serve to illustrate the range of style
encompassed by Tayma bichrome. It is entirely possible that
other as yet unrecognized stylistic phases are present, each
representing a different temporal span, the whole constituting
a ceramic tradition and a chronological continuum.

Conclusions

     This study has examined the painted pottery of the
northern Hejaz in its total occupational context through time
as revealed at the site of Tayma. Results suggest that this
pottery, rather than constituting a ceramic type which is
relatively homogeneous in its decoration and temporal span,
actually possesses a stylistic distribution and history which
is more complex than had been supposed. Pottery now usually
termed Midianite comprises the earliest style found at Tayma,
conforming to the accepted picture of a Midianite ceramic and
cultural distribution centered in the northern Hejaz and
extending north of the Gulf of 'Aqaba as an intrusive presence.
There is no firm evidence to dispute the generally-accepted
view that this Midianite pottery dates to the Late Bronze Age.

     The situation following the Midianite period is much more
complicated. While bichrome pottery from greater northwestern
Arabian sites, where it is associated with polychrome, has been
regarded as a component of Midianite ware, this designation does
not fit the occupational evidence at Tayma. There is abundant

indication of continuous settlement at Tayma at least from the
eighth century BC. However, every architectural feature which
can feasibly be dated by Assyrian and Neo-Babylonian texts and
archaeological evidence to this period is associated with
bichrome pottery similar in style to that previously regarded
as a sub-category of Midianite ware. These circumstances
strongly suggest that while some bichrome ware does indeed
date to the Late Bronze Age, it also represents a tradition
with continuous development extending through much of the 1st
millennium BC. Moreover it is clear that the nature of
stylistic development associated with this tradition is as yet
unknown, awaiting intensive ceramic study, although its terminal
point may well lay in the Khuraibah wares of the terminal Iron
Age.

The possibility of identifying sequential phases of
stylistic evolution in northwestern Arabian painted pottery
carries profound implications for future understanding of the
history of the region. First, such a situation will make
possible association of the known episodes of Assyrian and
Neo-Babylonian influence at Tayma with their material expressions.
Second, this association will in turn, through extrapolation to
other sites, facilitate identification of their histories. It
is to be expected that this exercise will reveal a more complex
occupational sequence at such important sites as Qurayyah,
which presently indicate a long chronological hiatus following
the Midianite period. In general a much clearer understanding
of the temporal parameters and stylistic denominators of
Midianite pottery and its successors should emerge. The
resulting culture historical framework based on integrated
ceramic and settlement studies will provide greatly enhanced
opportunity for relating regional developments with those of
the greater Near Eastern expressions of Late Bronze and Iron
Age civilizations.

BIBLIOGRAPHY

Bawden, Garth
1979   "Khief El-Zahrah and the Nature of Dedanite Hegemony
            in the Al 'Ula Oasis", *Atlal*, Vol. 3, pp. 63-72.
Bawden, Garth, Christopher Edens and Robert Miller
1980   "The Archaeological Resources of Ancient Tayma:
            Preliminary Investigations at Tayma", *Atlal*, Vol. 4,
            pp. 69-106.

Glueck, Nelson
1935   "Explorations in Eastern Palestine II", *Bulletin of
            the American Schools of Oriental Research,* 15.
1967   "Some Edomite Pottery from Tell El-Kheleifeh",
            Bulletin of the American Schools of Oriental Research,
            No. 188.
Parr, P.J., Harding, G.L. and Dayton, J.E.
1970   "Preliminary Survey in N.W. Arabia 1968", *Bulletin
            of the Institute of Archaeology, University of London,*
            Nos. 8 and 9.
Rothenberg, Beno
1972   *Timna.* Thames and Hudson.
Winnett, F.W. and Reed, W.L.
1970   *Ancient Records from North Arabia.* University of
            Toronto Press. Toronto.

THE EDOMITE POTTERY

M.F. Oakeshott
Institute of Archaeology
University of London
31-34 Gordon Square
London WC1H OPY

Iron Age pottery from Southern Jordan was first described by Dr Nelson Glueck in the 1930's following his comprehensive surveys, and was provisionally assigned by him to the early 13th to 8th century BC, though pre-eminently to Early Iron I, on the basis of both form and painted decoration (Glueck 1935). The painting is perhaps the most striking feature of this pottery, but it has turned out to be a deceptive indicator of date: excavations some 30 to 40 years after Glueck's pioneering work in Edom and elsewhere in Jordan have indicated that the Iron Age occupation of Southern Jordan is confined to the latter part of Iron II.

Four excavated sites in Southern Jordan have revealed Edomite pottery: Buseirah, Tawilan and Umm el-Biyara, all excavated by Mrs Crystal-M. Bennett, and, in the far south, Tell el-Kheleifeh, excavated by Dr Nelson Glueck. Through the kindness of Mrs Bennett the writer has been able to study the pottery from her sites, in particular Buseirah, and this paper will concentrate on these sites.

Buseirah in the late Iron Age was a substantial administrative centre dominated by two or three large buildings and fortified by a town wall (Bennett 1973, 1974, 1975, 1977). Tawilan has so far revealed only domestic buildings and appears to have been a minor settlement. The site is situated on a hillside sloping down to Petra,close to Wadi Musa (Bennett 1968, 1971). Umm el-Biyara lies within Petra, on the inaccessible summit of a nearly vertically-sided *massif*. As at Tawilan, no substantial buildings have been found (Bennett 1966). At each of these sites there is no sign of any occupation before about 800 BC. Not surprisingly, considering the size and nature of

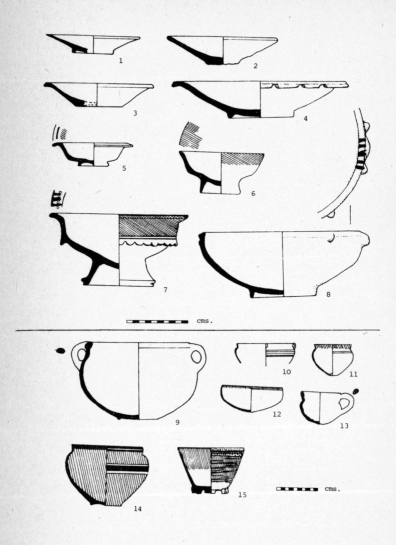

cms.

cms.

Figure 1

the site, the excavations at Buseirah have produced the largest
amount of pottery of the three sites. The chronological range
of occupation has not yet been fully established, but may
provisionally be taken to extend from the end of the 8th century
BC to the 6th century BC.

The most abundant vessel type from all phases of occupation
at Buseirah is the platter, a dish with sides flaring from the
base. It appears with ring, flat, rough or pedestal base, and
with a variety of rims from plain rounded to flanged and
denticulated (Fig. 1.1-4). Platters make up about 1/6 of all
pottery types from Buseirah. Next most common is a group of
carinated bowls with everted rims (Fig. 1.5) which occur in two
main versions: both types have an out-turned rim more or less
horizontal, but while one type is fairly deep the other is as
shallow as many of the platters. Both types may have flat or
ring bases, and in a few instances a pedestal base. This group
of bowls accounts for about 1/10 of the pottery from the site.
Another group of carinated bowls (Fig. 1.6) have the vessel wall
vertical above the carination; all these bowls have ring or
pedestal bases.

There is an important group of open bowls with triangular-
section rims. These bowls, often quite large (up to 40 cm in
rim diameter), almost invariably have ring bases, though
occasionally pedestal or tripod bases. Certain of them have a
horizontal bar handle, often flanked by a knob on each side, on
the exterior slightly below the rim (Fig. 1.8).

Deep bowls, or craters, with rim diameters around 30 cms
and two or four handles, are also common (Fig. 1.9). These
bowls always have a ring base. The position of the handle
varies: most have one end of the handle attached to the rim
and the other to the shoulder, but in a few instances the handle
is applied below the rim.

A very abundant deep bowl type has a short vertical neck
above a rounded body (Fig. 1.14). These bowls usually have a
ring base but are also found with flat bases.

One group of bowls is characterised by exceptionally thin
walls, often only 2 mm in thickness (Fig. 1.10, 11, 12).
Despite the delicacy of the walls, some of these bowls have rim
diameters up to 20 cms, though most are between 8 and 15 cms.
The weakest point of the vessels, as is so often the case, is

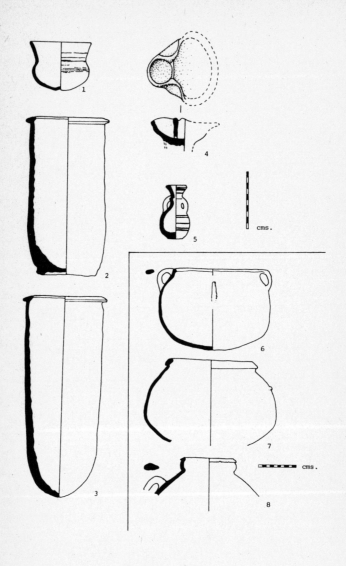

Figure 2

the joint between wall and base, and very few bases have
survived. Within this group are three types, one with rounded
sides and base and flaring or vertical rim (Fig. 1.10 and 11);
one with rounded sides and rim continuing the line of the wall;
and the third with carination (Fig. 1.12). All bowls in this
group were not only shaped with extreme care but have finely
finished surfaces and meticulously applied paint, and have been
described as "fine ware".

Equally well finished, but with walls of normal thickness,
is a group of cups or beakers with rounded or dimpled bases
and flaring rims (Fig. 2.1). Some types in this group are
shallow, consisting mainly of flaring wall and rim; others are
quite deep (as Fig. 2.1). None of these beakers has a handle,
but another group of drinking vessels with rounded base and
flaring rim does have handles (Fig. 1.13): these mugs are
roughly made and finished. Another group of small vessels
presumably also used for drinking resembles flower pots except
for the absence of a drainage hole (Fig. 1.15). These vessels
are as carefully finished as the flaring-rimmed beakers, and
have either tripod or rounded bases.

One group of bowls or perhaps chalices from Buseirah is
characterised not only by form but by the distinctive fabric
from which it is made, a white-firing clay. These vessels, of
which none of the relatively few found has a base, have rounded
sides and flaring rims and a loop handle from the rim to the
body (possibly two handles symmetrically arranged).

Bowls, platters, and small drinking vessels between them
make up nearly half the pottery excavated at Buseirah. The
remainder, cooking pots, jugs, jars, lamps and miscellaneous,
can be dealt with briefly. To begin with cooking pots. The
two commonest types have probably two or more handles attached
at the rim and the shoulder, and a ridge on the outside of the
rim: in one type the line of the rim continues the line of the
body; in the other type there is a short vertical neck. A few
examples of other types have been found, one with a distinct
neck bearing two or three ridges with a handle from the rim to
the shoulders; one with a kind of bow-rim terminating in a
triangular section rim, with a handle at the shoulder (Fig. 2.8);
one with an almost square rim, between loop handles from rim to
shoulder, a vertical bar applied to the wall at the shoulder, or
no loop handles and a horizontal bar above the shoulder
(Fig. 2.6); one with a rim shaped like one of the deep bowl

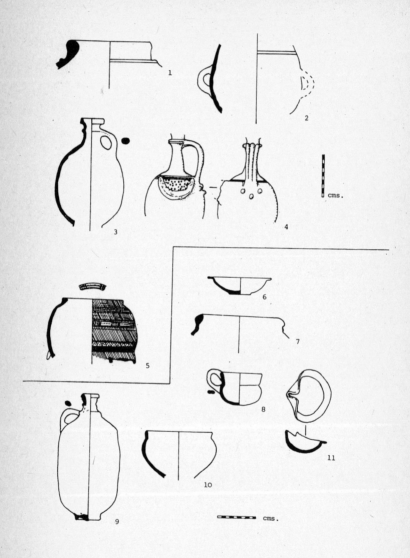

Figure 3

types (cf. Fig. 1.9), with no handles but a knob at the shoulder (Fig. 2.7).

Although there is a wide range of jar and jug types at Buseirah, relatively few complete or reconstructable vessels were found and in only a few cases is there more than one identifiable example of a type. The jars include large heavy pithoi (Fig. 3.1) as well as smaller jars with ovoid bodies (Fig. 3.2). The commonest jar type is a coarse cylindrical vessel (Fig. 2.2 and 3): large quantities of these, mainly broken, were found in a few provenances. The rims are usually everted and the bases either round or roughly flattened. These jars presumably held a particular commodity either made or stored in quantity at Buseirah.

The commonest jug type has an ovoid body, a neck with a ridged rim but no lip, and a handle from the shoulder to the rim. The base is either round or a ring. The decanter type of jug, with the handle attached at a ridge encircling the neck, also appears (Fig. 3.3). Interesting though uncommon types are locally-made imitations of juglets of Cypro-Mycenaean type (Fig. 2.5) and a jug made only in white-firing clay with plastic detail imitating metal forms (Fig. 3.4).

Lamps with rounded bases, stump bases and pedestals were found at Buseirah. One type of lamp, of which there are several examples, has a partition dividing the lip from the body of the lamp, and seems to have had a pedestal base, though none of this type survived complete (Fig. 2.4).

The painted decoration, which forms such a conspicuous feature of the pottery from Buseirah, appears on approximately half the bowls and a number of jars and jugs. The paint used was pigmented slip, applied to the vessel before firing and adhering well to the surface. The slips fired red, brown or black and, less commonly, white, and were most often painted in horizontal lines and bands (e.g. Fig. 1.14). On broad-rimmed vessels, short parallel strokes are often painted in groups across the rim (Fig. 1.8, 3.5). On a few vessels more elaborate geometrical designs were used: blobs and spots, saltires, cross-hatching, panel designs, and variants of vertical and horizontal lines (e.g. Fig. 3.5).

Plastic decoration also occurs. The commonest and most effective type is the denticulated band at the rim of certain

platters and bowls and at the carinations of some bowls (Fig. 1.4
and 7, Fig. 3.5). The denticulations were made by cutting away
clay from the rim or a separate strip of clay to be applied at
the carination: the knife marks are clearly visible. Impressed
dots and thumb impressions were occasionally used. Seal
impressions were found on two fine-ware bowls: both impressions
are rectangular and one is of a cow suckling a calf, the other
of a stag.

Red slip plus burnishing is uncommon, though it does occur,
and almost never covers the whole surface of a vessel. Where
burnishing is used it is generally restricted to the painted
bands of red slip and consists of a few distinct lines, roughly
horizontal, presumably for decorative effect alone. Certain
platters were treated by a technique which resembles burnishing:
these vessels were shaped by turning away excess clay from the
interior, followed by smoothing, and this treatment has left
smooth spiral bands 3-5 mm broad. Vessels finished in this way
are always left unpainted.

Analysis of the pottery fabrics from Buseirah is in
progress. From visual examination certain characteristics have
been identified. The clays normally fire within the range
red-buff-orange-grey, though white firing clays were also used.
The clay matrix contains a considerable quantity of calcareous
material which effectively prevents firing above about 900°C.
The maximum temperature in the kiln was reached quickly and
maintained for a fairly short time, and thicker sherds (5 mm
and above) nearly always have a grey or black unoxidised core.
Many pots exhibit a variety of surface colours, not infrequently
almost the whole range possible from the clay. Inclusions used
are basalt, quartz, grog, mica, vegetable matter, and the
ubiquitous calcite. A grey-green firing basaltic clay was used
for a majority of large jugs but was not restricted to this type;
a white-firing clay with few discernible inclusions was used for
a handled drinking-vessel and a jug (Fig. 3.4); cooking pots
were invariably made from a highly siliceous clay.

The pottery assemblage from Tawilan is virtually identical
to that from Buseirah. Most of the Tawilan pottery is less
well finished than most of the Buseirah pottery: inclusions tend
to be larger, and more surface damage was caused in firing; but
the pottery is as often painted and with the same range of
motifs. Denticulations are less common at Tawilan, and tend to
be cut with less precision than at Buseirah. One technique for

shaping pots used at Tawilan does not appear at Buseirah:
handleless flaring-rim drinking cups are sometimes dimpled by
thumb impressions on the exterior.

From Umm el-Biyara the assemblage is rather different,
though there are parallels with vessels from Buseirah and
Tawilan. Some of the jar rims occur at Buseirah (Fig. 3.4).
The decanter type of jug (Fig. 3.9) is only a distant relation
of the Buseirah decanters; one Umm el-Biyara variant on this
type has concave sides and is noticeably wider at the shoulder
than at the carination above the base (for this vessel the only
parallel known at present is from the Tomb of Adoni Nur, in
Amman). However, one Umm el-Biyara jug with a ridge below the
rim is identical to the commonest type of jug from Buseirah.
Few of the bowls have close parallels at Buseirah, though there
is a deep bowl or crater with folded everted rim which is close
to a common Buseirah type. A thin-walled bowl with loop
handles flanked by knobs recalls the Buseirah fine-ware bowls,
but differs from all Buseirah examples in its angular shape.
Platters were found at Umm el-Biyara, as were everted-rim bowls
(Fig. 6.3), both types common at Buseirah. The mugs with
handles from Umm el-Biyara (Fig. 3.8) also parallel the
Buseirah mugs. There is a crudely-made version of the flaring-
rim beakers found at Buseirah (cf. Fig. 2.1). Lids, which may
of course equally serve as platters, are similar to some lids
and the rougher platter types from Buseirah. The deep bowl with
neck (Fig. 3.10) is exactly paralleled by a common Buseirah
type. The lamps (e.g. Fig. 3.11) are of types found at
Buseirah, but there is a tendency for Umm el-Biyara lamps to
be deeper: Buseirah has a much shallower type than any lamps
from Umm el-Biyara.

Precise dating of these Edomite sites is not at present
possible: this area still remains somewhat enigmatic in its
relationships with neighbouring cultures. When the Edomite
pottery assemblages are compared, 85% of vessel types from
Tawilan can be closely paralleled with vessels from Buseirah,
and 68% of the Umm el-Biyara types have parallels at Buseirah.
From Tell el-Kheleifeh Level IV (published material only) 83%
is paralleled at Buseirah. It is not within the scope of this
paper to go into detail in listing dated ceramic parallels to
the Edomite pottery, but some general comments may be made.
Ceramic parallels with other Iron II sites in Jordan (Dhiban,
the Mount Nebo tombs, Heshbon, the tombs in the Amman area) are
numerous, and substantiate the picture of a distinctive East

Jordanian pottery assemblage. Within the major assemblage the
minor Edomite group has many of its own features, not only in
vessel forms but also in the use of painted and plastic
decoration: both types of decoration, while not uncommon in
central and northern Transjordanian Iron II assemblages, seem
to be most characteristic of the Edomite sites, where they occur
with far greater profusion and on a wider range of vessel types.
Parallels of form and decoration from Palestine are extensive,
but few are of help in refining the chronology of the East
Jordanian sites. The decoration in particular causes more
problems than it solves as the range of proliferation of painted
motifs on the Edomite pottery recalls the Late Bronze Age rather
than later Iron II. Evidence for dating some groups has been
provided by seals and seal impressions. From Umm el-Biyara there
is the seal of Qos Gabr, dated to the 7th century. 16% of the
vessel types from this southern site, including some forms
confined to these two groups, have parallels from the Tomb of
Adoni Nur in Amman, in which was found the seal of Adoni Nur,
dated to c.650 BC. Qws ^{c}nl seal impressions from Kheleifeh Level
IV were dated to the 7th-6th centuries. One pottery form
strengthens the case for a 7th century date: the flaring-rim
beaker with rounded base, which in Palestine first appears in
levels associated with an Assyrian presence at the end of the
8th century and in the 7th century, is known at Buseirah,
Tawilan and Tell-el-Kheleifeh, with a crude version from Umm
el-Biyara.

There remain a number of vessel types which appear to be
unique to Edom, such as the flower-pot shaped beakers and the
lamps with internal partitions from Buseirah. These strange
vessels, and the cheerful habit of painting a high proportion
of all pots made, could simply be a local cultural development
in a somewhat isolated region. It seems probable, however,
that the isolation exists only as viewed from the west of the
Wadi Arabah, and that as more archaeological exploration takes
place in the areas to the south and east of Edom the Iron II
pottery of this land will be seen as part of an extensive
regional tradition.

SELECTED BIBLIOGRAPHY

Bennett, C.-M.   "Fouilles d'Umm el-Biyara", *Revue Biblique* 73 (1966), pp. 372-391.

Bennett, C.-M.   "The Excavations at Tawilan, near Petra", *Annual of the Department of Antiquities of Jordan* XII-XIII (1967-68), pp. 53-55.

Bennett, C.-M.   "A brief note on excavations at Tawilan, 1968-70", *Levant* 3 (1971), pp. v-vii.

Bennett, C.-M.   "Excavations at Buseirah, Southern Jordan 1971: a preliminary report", *Levant* 5 (1973), pp. 1-11.

Bennett, C.-M.   "Excavations at Buseirah, Southern Jordan 1972: a preliminary report", *Levant* 6 (1974), pp. 1-24.

Bennett, C.-M.   "Excavations at Buseirah, Southern Jordan: third preliminary report", *Levant* 7 (1975), pp. 1-19.

Bennett, C.-M.   "Excavations at Buseirah, Southern Jordan: fourth preliminary report", *Levant* 9 (1977), pp. 1-10.

Glueck, N.   "Explorations in Eastern Palestine II", *Annual of the American School of Oriental Research* XV (1935).

Glueck, N.   "Some Edomite Pottery from Tell el-Kheleifeh", *Bulletin of the American Schools of Oriental Research* 188 (1967).

Harding, G.L.   "Four Tomb Groups from Jordan IV: The Tomb of Adoni Nur in Amman", *Palestine Exploration Fund Annual* VI (1953), pp. 37-40.

Oakeshott, M.F.   *A Study of the Iron Age II Pottery of East Jordan with Special Reference to Unpublished Material from Edom.*   (Unpublished doctoral thesis, University of London, 1978).

THE MIDIANITE POTTERY

Beno Rothenberg and Jonathan Glass
Institute of Archaeology
University of London
31-34 Gordon Square
London WC1H OPY

Introduction

During surveys and excavations in the south-western 'Arabah between 1959 and 1966 a pottery group unique in material and fabrication techniques as well as in vessel types and decorations was identified. Despite the large number of sherds of this group found in the 'Arabah, scholars were perplexed about both their exact dating and provenance. In 1969, one of the present authors (B.R.) examined at the Institute of Archaeology of the University of London a collection of sherds collected not long before in an archaeological survey in N.W. Arabia, a region generally identified with biblical Midian; that collection contained many sherds closely resembling those of the 'Arabah noted above. As a result it was proposed that Midian be considered the country of origin of this pottery /1/.

In the present paper we shall present the Midianite pottery, define its characteristics, consider the archaeological basis for its dating and prove that it in fact originated in Midian. We shall not deal here with the culture-historical significance of the appearance of the Midianite pottery nor with its ethnological or biblical aspects /2/.

1. First Finds and the Timna' Excavations (Fig. 1)

1.1 'Arabah Survey

The first 'Arabah survey, conducted in 1959-60 by the "'Arabah Expedition" headed by B. Rothenberg, found a few decorated sherds in various places in the 'Arabah - in the northern 'Arabah on the Dead Sea coast (Mesad Gozal), in the southern 'Arabah (especially in the Timna' valley but also in

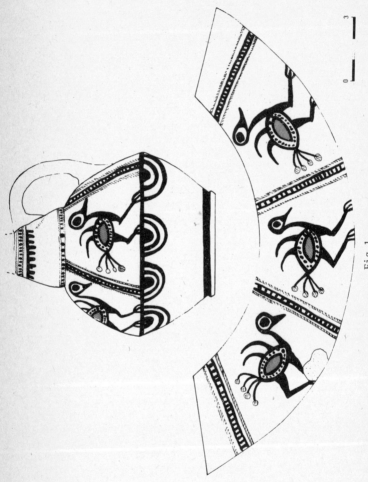

Fig.1

Midianite juglet from Southern Jordan (exact provenance unknown).

Nahal Shlomo - Site No. 86 on the ʿArabah Survey map), and on
"Coral Island" (Jezirat Fara'un) /3/.

A comparison of these Arabah sherds with decorated pottery
from Eastern Palestine (Edom) described by N. Glueck /4/ showed
a close resemblance in the decorations, and consequently the
decorated pottery from the ʿArabah sites was identified as
"Edomite" pottery /5/. At that preliminary stage of the ʿArabah
explorations, before any of the Timna' sites had been excavated,
this "Edomite" pottery was dated according to the other pottery
groups found together with it at various sites in the area -
hand-made "Negev pottery" and ordinary wheel-made pottery - to
about the tenth century BC /6/. Undoubtedly "that dating was
largely influenced by the generally held view that we are dealing
with King Solomon's Mines and by the reluctance of scholars to
accept even such an early date" /7/.

1.2   The Timna' Excavations, Site No. 2, 1964, 1966

In 1964 and 1966, Smelting Camp No. 2 was excavated /8/ and
a relatively large quantity of decorated pottery found. The
excavations showed that the three groups of pottery found during
the surface survey - the "Edomite", "Negev" and the "ordinary" -
appeared together at all levels of the site. However, the
decorated "Edomite" pottery was now dated to Iron Age I /9/, to
the twelfth century BC at the latest /10/. This was done on the
basis of the "ordinary" pottery, including cooking pots uncovered
here for the first time /11/, and of two scarabs of the XIX
Dynasty and a toggle-pin of an early type, found in excavation.

The excavations at Site No. 2 produced geometric decorations
much more sophisticated than the characteristic Edomite
decorations published by N. Glueck, or found in recent years
by C. Bennett in her excavations in Jordan, the latter consisting
mainly of straight lines around the vessel or a net-decoration
all over it. However, since decorations similar to those of
Site No. 2 /12/ had been called "Edomite" by N. Glueck,
attention was not then directed at the significant differences
between the Timna' and Edomite sherds. However, stressing that
"the ceramic and metallurgical finds of Timna' should not be
related to Palestine in general nor to the Kingdom of Israel in
particular", we continued to relate the decorated pottery of
Timna' to the kings of Edom /13/.

The many uncertainties and discussions regarding the
identification and date of the decorated Timna' pottery mainly

resulted from the fact that the comparisons were made solely on
the basis of N. Glueck's quite general descriptions and his
drawings and photographs. If it had been possible at the time
to compare the pottery itself, it would no doubt have been
evident at an earlier stage that there was no real resemblance
between the "Edomite" pottery and that now termed "Midianite" -
not in shape, material, pottery technique or decorations.

1.3   The Timna' Sanctuary

In the summer of 1969, an Egyptian shrine /14/ (Site No.
200) was uncovered in the Timna' valley, and decorated pottery
was found in layers II and III, the principal layers of the
shrine. The decorated pottery of Site No. 200 constituted 25%
of all the pottery found and consisted mainly of small delicate
vessels, apparently offerings to Hathor. Especially notable
were the numerous vessels decorated with complicated geometrical
designs in black, red and brown and with drawings of ostriches
and a strange-looking human figure. The same three groups of
pottery, found together during the survey and in the sealed
layers of Site No. 2, were also found at the Timna' Sanctuary,
but here numerous Egyptian objects and inscriptions were found
as well.

The first petrographic examination of the Timna' Sanctuary
pottery, made in 1969, right at the end of the excavations,
indicated that the decorated pottery "differs in clay and
temper from any pottery known from Palestine and Syria"/15/.

According to its stratified context, the decorated pottery
discussed here belongs to the 19th and 20th Egyptian Dynasties,
i.e. from the thirteenth century BC to the middle of the twelfth
century BC /16/.

1.4   The Identification of the Midianite Pottery

In the summer of 1969 B. Rothenberg lectured at the
Institute of Archaeology of the University of London on the
discovery of the Egyptian miners' sanctuary at Timna', and Peter
Parr, who took part in the subsequent discussion, noted that at
the Institute there exists a collection of sherds from a recent
survey in the Hejaz, which contains many sherds closely
resembling the decorated Timna' pottery. Already the initial
examination of these Hejaz sherds /17/ showed that there was no
difference at all between the group of sherds from Kh. Qurayyah
and the decorated pottery from Timna'. Among the identical

decorations were those of birds and the strange human figure as well as sophisticated geometrical designs. Just like Timna', particularly at Site No. 2, the Hejaz had also produced undecorated sherds whose ceramic properties were identical to those of the decorated ones. The resemblances were typological as well, both collections having the identical deep bowls and goblets with beautiful decorations and small shallow bowls decorated both inside and outside. Already at that stage of our research it was reasonable to assume that the decorated pottery of Timna' had originated from Midian and it was therefore proposed to name it "Midianite pottery" /18/. As Egyptian inscriptions dated the pottery of the Timna' Sanctuary to the 19th and 20th Dynasties, the Midianite pottery must have been in use at least from the end of the fourteenth century BC to the middle of the twelfth century BC.

2. Distribution and Chronology of the Midianite Pottery (Fig. 2)

In recent years, following the first publication of the identity of the Midianite pottery, similar pottery has been identified at various sites of Arabia (Midian), Jordan (Edom), the ʿArabah, Israel and northern Sinai. Wherever possible, these sherds were examined by the authors /19/ and their identification confirmed, but our distribution map also lists some isolated finds as well as groups classified as "Midianite" by their excavators, which have not been examined petrographically. Following is a list of the sites from which Midianite pottery was reported, together with their archaeological context, the characteristics and identity of the sherds as well as their dating.

2.1 N.W. Arabia (Hejaz)

2.1.1 Qurayyah - about 70 km north-west of Tabuk

Publications: P.J. Parr, G.L. Harding, J.E. Dayton, *Bull. Inst. of Arch.* 8-9 (London, 1970), 219-241, pls. 39-40, 42; J.E. Dayton, *Proc. Seminar for Arabian Studies* (London, 1972), 25-37.

A survey in Midian, conducted by Parr, Harding and Dayton in 1968, uncovered a large quantity of sherds which were classified into eighteen groups on the basis of material and shape. The scholars noted in particular the homogeneity in material of the Qurayyah pottery of all groups, which, except for a few examples of fine-grained clay with very few grits, was made of "coarse or medium wares, varying in colours from light

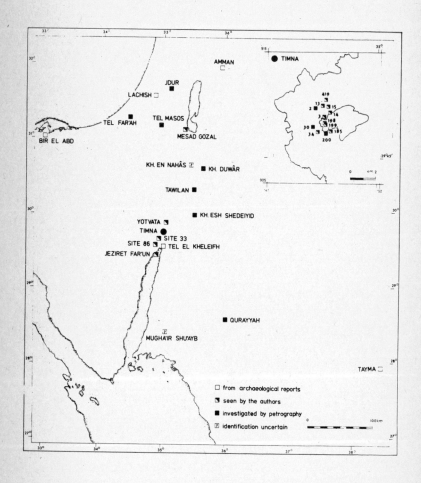

Fig. 2
Distribution map of Midianite pottery

red through pink and buff, to cream" (Parr *et al.*, 238).
According to Parr *et al.* most of the vessels were wheel-made,
but there were also some coil and hand-built vessels.
Undecorated vessels were usually covered with a thick slip
of a darker colour than the fabric. Especially outstanding
was the pottery decorated in two colours. The decoration,
generally on a light brown or yellowish background, was in
tints of black, brown, red and yellow. The decorations were
mainly geometrical, but there were also some drawings of animals
and birds (Parr *et al.*, 238: illustrations 15-18; pl. 42). The
investigators proposed dating the decorated pottery to the
"final centuries of the second millennium BC" /20/. The
importance of the Qurayyah finds lies in the discovery of a
facility there for the production of the decorated pottery, so
that evidently Qurayyah was a centre of the Midianite ceramic
industry (Parr *et al.*, 240, pls. 34-40).

A petrographic examination was made of a representative
sample of the several hundred sherds of Qurayyah pottery at
London University's Institute of Archaeology /21/ including
both decorated and undecorated sherds (Thin Sections - No.
1108-1113, 1134, 1138, 1211). We could not find in the London
collection all the groups (A-N) described by P. Parr *et al.*,
and it was hard to determine from the published drawings alone
exactly which of the groups occur in the collection. As already
noted by Dayton (*ibid.*, 1972, 28) only some of the pottery
groups found at Qurayyah were identical with the decorated and
undecorated Midianite pottery found at Timna' (TS 1108, 1110,
1112, 1113). However, according to our examination (see below)
all the Qurayyah pottery groups in the London collection were
made of the same material - matrix and temper - even if they
differ completely in all other aspects and seem to belong to
different periods. For example, TS 1109, 1111 and 1134
represented pottery groups not found at Timna' or anywhere
else besides Qurayyah, which also completely differed in shape.
Yet, these vessels were all made of the same type of matrix and
temper from which the groups identical with the Timna' pottery
were made.

An exception is a group of small delicate vessels - only
sherds of which were in the London collection, making an exact
definition of types impossible - made of fine-grained white
clay with very small grits and with fine burnished creamy
surface. One of these sherds was inscribed "Mycenae" so that
it apparently belonged with group E or F which Dayton (*ibid.*, 29)
related to Mycenaean pottery. Its petrographic examination

showed that it was made at Qurayyah (see TS 1211, 1138) and was not imported. As such pottery was also found at the Timna' Sanctuary (TS 1106), it must be considered a sub-group of the Midianite pottery of the 19th and 20th Dynasties.

2.1.2 Tayma - about 300 km south-east of Qurayyah and
       120 km north-east of Medā'in Saliḥ.

Publications: F.V. Winnett, W.L. Reed, *Ancient Records from North Arabia* (Toronto 1970), 175, pl. 84; P. Parr, G.L. Harding, J.E. Dayton, "Preliminary Survey in N.W. Arabia 1968", *Bull. Inst. of Arch.* 8-9 (1970), 240; G. Bawden, C. Edens, R. Miller, *Atlal* 4 (Riyadh, 1980), 69-106.

A survey conducted in 1962 by Winnett and Reed uncovered among many sherds of different groups and different periods /22/ several fragments of decorated small shallow bowls and of one deep bowl (Figs. 84, 2, 3, 7), which look like Midianite pottery. By comparison with pottery from the Dibon excavations and Nelson Glueck's publications, the investigators dated this pottery, with some reservations, to Iron Age I and II (see Winnett and Reed, *ibid.*, 175). At the Riyadh Museum Mr Parr's team examined sacks of sherds purportedly from Tayma and found among them a large number belonging to the Midianite pottery group (Parr *et al.*, 240) /23/.

During a detailed survey of Tayma in 1979, Bawden, Edens and Miller collected a large number of sherds which were classified into "three discrete ceramic assemblages". Typology I: "Iron Age painted and undecorated wares roughly comparable to the ceramics known from both Qurayyah and the al-'Ula sites (Khuraybah) in form and decorations" was dated "to the first six centuries of the 1st millennium BC and perhaps earlier still (Bawden *et al.*, 89). There is no doubt that proper Midianite pottery appears in Bawden's "Typology I" of Tayma, identical in shape, decorations and, apparently, material, with the Midianite pottery from Qurayyah and Timna'. Unfortunately Bawden *et al.* did not realise that their "Typology I" consists of at least two essentially different wares of completely different origin and date: Midianite ware, as found in Qurayyah, Timna, etc., dated by Ramesside inscriptions to the 13th-12th centuries BC (see below 2.3.1), and "Khuraybah ware" (see below 2.7.1) of so far unknown origin and seemingly much later date. It is unfortunate that this mix-up of totally different pottery groups resulted in a rather unacceptable temporal range of about one millennium for

the Tayma pottery of "Typology I-Iron Age" (see also below 2.2.5).
Bawden *et al.* seem to date their pottery groups by historical
considerations rather than by straightforward archaeological
evidence and as far as their "Typology I" is concerned, this
method has caused a mix-up of obviously Late Bronze (Midianite)
and Iron Age (Khuraybah) pottery groups.

2.1.3 Mugha'ir Shu'ayb-Al-Bad' - about 30 km east of Maqna.

Publications: P. Parr, G.L. Harding, J.E. Dayton, *op. cit.* 8-9
(1970) 240; id., "Preliminary Survey (contd.)", *Bull. Inst. of
Arch.* 10, (1972), 33.

Extensive ruins were found near the Nabataean burials of
Mugha'ir Shu'ayb, next to the village of al-Bad', which many
investigators believed to have been a huge Nabataean city
(P. Parr *et al., op. cit.,* 10 (1972), 33). During the survey
by Parr's team, a great many sherds were found, all of them
Nabataean-Roman and later. Their report (*op. cit.,* 8-9 (1970),
240) mentioned one sherd that may belong to the Midianite
pottery. In Part Two of this report (1972, 33) this sherd was
further discussed and was found to be similar to the undecorated
ware from Qurayyah. The authors refer to Figs. 17 and 18 of
their report, but those figures include primarily sherds which,
by their shape and appearance, do not belong to the Midianite
pottery group. We included this sherd, which was published
without detailed description, and could not be petrographically
examined, in our distribution map with some reservation.
However, it should be remembered that roughly-made vessels
without decoration found at Timna' /24/ proved upon petrographic
examination to belong to the Midianite pottery group.

2.2 The ʿArabah and the Gulf of ʿAqabah - Eilat

2.2.1 Mesad Gozal (formerly Umm Zoghal) - G.R. 1866 0604 -
       a ruin on the shores of the Dead Sea.

Publications: Y. Aharoni-B. Rothenberg, *Be-Ikvot Malakhim
ve-Mordim* (Tel Aviv, 1960), 16-17; B. Rothenberg, *Tsefunot
Negev* (Tel Aviv, 1967), 113-114; Y. Aharoni, *IEJ* 14 (1964),
112-113.

During the first examination of the site in 1957 by
B. Rothenberg (Site No. 49 on the ʿArabah Survey map) only very
few sherds were found, among them five decorated body sherds
which could not then be identified. Following the discovery in

1959 of the decorated pottery in Timna', the Mesad Gozal sherds
were seen to belong to the same group, designated as "Edomite"
and dated to Iron Age I (Rothenberg, 1967, 114).

Excavating the site in 1964, Y. Aharoni found pottery but
no additional decorated sherds. He proposed to see the small
site as an Edomite tower-like fortlet, dating to the 11th-10th
cent. BC (Aharoni, *IEJ*, 14 (1964), -113). In view of the
identification of Mesad Gozal's decorated pottery as Midianite,
and in the absence of any evidence for a date later than the
twelfth century BC for this pottery, the date of the construction
of Mesad Gozal should also be pushed back. The Mesad Gozal
pottery was not examined petrographically /25/.

2.2.2 The Yotvata Fortress (formerly 'Ayn el-Ghadian): GR 1553 9225.

Publications: B. Rothenberg, *Tsefunot Negev* (1967), 140-142;
Z. Meshel, *Toldot ha-Negev be-Tkufat Malkei Israel,* unpublished
doctoral dissertation (Tel Aviv, 1974), 3-4, 83, fig. 17; *id.,*
Hadashot Arkeologiyot 91-92 (1974), 38-39; 96 (1975), 50-51;
94-95 (1975), 34-35; N. Glueck, *BASOR* 145 (1957), 23-25; *id.,*
Rivers in the Desert (1959), 36-37; Z. Meshel, *RB* 84 (1977),
267, pl. IXc. See also J. Kalsbeek, G. London, *BASOR*, 232 (1978),
47-56.

The site was first described by Glueck and, on the basis of
pottery found on the surface, he dated the site to the Iron Age
II, to the time of "King Solomon's Mines" (1959, 36). During
B. Rothenberg's ᶜArabah survey (1967, 140) the fortress (Site
No. 44 on the ᶜArabah Survey map) was dated to the Iron Age I.
No decorated pottery was found on the surface during that survey.
In his first publications, the excavator, Z. Meshel, identified
the Yotvata site as an "Israelite Fortress" and dated it to the
tenth century (*Toldot ha-Negev,* 3-4). In 1974-75, in his
excavations of Yotvata, Meshel found three groups of pottery:
handmade Negev ware, ordinary wheel-made pottery and two large
sherds of Midianite vessels. In view of the date of the
Midianite pottery from the Timna' Sanctuary, Meshel now dates
the fortress to the 13th-12th cent. BC /26/. Among the Yotvata
finds was a small bowl decorated both inside and outside and a
large fragment of a deep bowl /27/ with geometric decorations
typical of Midianite pottery. Unfortunately, we could not
examine these sherds petrographically, but their visual
examination showed them definitely to belong to the Midianite
group.

2.2.3   Site No. 33, Nahal 'Amran (formerly Wadi 'Amrani):
        GR 1438 8956

Publications: I. Braslawi, *Hayadata et ha-Aretz*, 4 (1956), 327;
B. Rothenberg, *Tsefunot Negev* (1967), 44-47, fig. 22; N. Glueck,
BA (1959), 91; *id.*, *BASOR*, 159 (1960), 12-14; B. Rothenberg,
PEQ, 94 (1962), 37-38.

A number of decorated sherds, resembling the Timna' pottery
in shape and decoration, were found at a copper smelting camp
(Site No. 3 on the 'Arabah Survey map) in the Nahal 'Amran and,
accordingly, dated to the 13th-12th centuries BC.

2.2.4   Site No. 86, in Nahal Shlomo (formerly Wadi Masri)
        alongside the Ma'aleh Eilat (formerly Nagb el 'Aqaba):
        GR 1391 8871. See the 'Arabah Survey map, appendix to
        the Eloth Survey, Israel Survey Department, Tel Aviv,
        1967.

Publications: B. Rothenberg, *Tsefunot Negev,* 1967, 157-158.

At a camping site, dated on the basis of pottery finds to
Iron Age I, a number of sherds decorated in black and red on a
creamy slip were found in 1959; they resembled those "found in
the smelting camps of the Timna valley, at Jezirat Fara'un and
in other places in the 'Arabah" (Rothenberg, 1967, 158).

2.2.5   Tel el-Kheleifeh, on the Red Sea coast, in the Gulf of
        'Aqaba-Eilat: GR 147 8842.

Publications: N. Glueck, *AASOR*, XV (1935), 124-137; *id.*, *BASOR*,
188 (1967), 10-14; *id.*, *Eretz Israel*, IX (1969), 51-54; *id.*, *BA*,
28 (1964), 70-87.

Glueck's publications before 1959 on the Tel el-Kheleifeh
excavations did not mention decorated pottery of the group
discussed here /28/. In 1959, in an article by G.A. Wright /29/
appeared for the first time the photograph of a jug with
geometric decorations similar to the Midianite designs. This
jug was dated to Iron Age II. The same jug was published again
in 1967, together with other pottery, in Nelson Glueck's
"Edomite Pottery from Tel el-Kheleifeh" (*BASOR* 188 (1967), 10).
On the basis of its assumed stratigraphic location in Stratum IV
of Tel el-Kheleifeh it was dated by Glueck to Late Iron Age II,
that is, "not earlier than the late eighth century and not later

than the sixth century BC" /30/.   Fig. 1:2 of the article
showed the jug from Tel el-Kheleifeh (see also fig. 5:1A) and
a similar jug found at Timna' many years ago /31/. Both appear
to belong to the Midianite pottery group. Fig. 4:2-5 included
among other decorated pottery four sherds from Tel el-Kheleifeh
which bear Midianite pottery decorations. They too, according
to Glueck, were found in Layer IV, "in the seventh to sixth
century BC".

On the basis of their appearance, we tend to consider those
sherds (Fig. 1:1-2 and 4:2-5) as belonging to the Midianite
group, dating, according to the Timna' Sanctuary, to the period
from the beginning of the thirteenth to mid-twelfth cent. BC.
It is hard to accept such a longevity of such homogeneous
pottery, from the thirteenth to the sixth cent. BC, that is,
some seven hundred years. It is more reasonable to assume that
on Glueck's figures, including Fig. 2 of the above mentioned
article, there appeared two different pottery groups: decorated
"Edomite" sherds of the 8th-7th cent. BC /32/ and Midianite
sherds which, according to the Timna' finds, must be dated to the
13th-12th cent. BC /33/. It must be borne in mind that,
according to Glueck, Midianite pottery appeared in Tel
el-Kheleifeh not in the tenth cent. BC but in the seventh or
sixth, when it was an Edomite city, and also that no pottery
from Tel el-Kheleifeh earlier than the eighth cent. BC has ever
been published. To date not a single sherd has been published
from the excavations of Tel el-Kheleifeh which dates to King
Solomon's time and it is doubtful whether the site was at all
inhabited during the period of the United Kingdom of Israel and
Judah /34/. At the same time, the Midianite sherds found at or
near Tel el-Kheleifeh - apparently on the surface - attest to
the probable existence of a pre-Israelite settlement related to
13th-12th cent. BC Midian.

2.2.6 Jezirat Fara'un (Coral Island) in the Gulf of 'Aqaba-Eilat;
       GR 1363 8749.

Publications: Tagliyot Sinai (Tel Aviv, 1952), 169-174; Tsefunot
Negev (Tel Aviv, 1967), 207-213; B. Rothenberg, God's Wilderness
(London, 1961), 86-92; id., Timna (London, 1972), 202-207;
A. Flinder, Intern. J. of Nautical Arch., 6 (1977), 127-139.

In the course of a short trip to the island in 1957,
B. Rothenberg gathered a number of decorated sherds, including
a fragment of a juglet and body sherds of a deep bowl (1967, 211,

fig. no. 268), which could not then be identified or dated
because of the lack of suitable comparisons. After the
discovery of numerous decorated sherds in the Timna' valley, a
comparison with the sherds from the island was made, revealing
great similarity between the two finds groups (see Rothenberg,
1961, 91, n.2). As the sherds from the island were surface
finds, they cannot be dated independently, but following their
identification as Midianite pottery they should be related to
the 13th-12th cent. BC.

2.3 The Timna' Valley (formerly Wadi Mene'iyeh) (see insert in fig. 2).

Publications: B. Rothenberg and A. Lupu, *Museum Ha'aretz
Bulletin*, 7 (Tel Aviv, 1965), 19-28: 9 (1967), 53-70:
B. Rothenberg, *Tsefunot Negev* (1967), 3-41: *id.*, *Museum
Ha'aretz Bulletin*, 12 (1970), 28-35: *id.*, *Hadashot Arkeologiyot*,
94-95 (1975), 33-34; *id.*, *ILN*, Arch. 2323 (15.6.1969), Arch.
2324 (29.9.1969); *id.*, *Bible et Terre Sainte*, 139 (1970), 6-14;
A. Lupu and B. Rothenberg, *Arch. Austriaca*, 47 (1970), 91-130;
P.J. Parr, G.L. Harding, J.E. Dayton, *Bull. Inst. of Arch.*, 8-9
(London, 1970), 230-240; B. Rothenberg, *Timna* (London, 1972);
H.G. Conrad - B. Rothenberg (eds.), *Antikes Kupfer im Timna-Tal*
(Bochum, 1980).

Between 1964 and 1976, three smelting camps were excavated
in the Timna' valley, and at all three sites Midianite pottery
was found in the layers of the New Egyptian Kingdom, dated, on
the basis of finds at Site No. 200 (the Egyptian-Midianite
Sanctuary of Timna'), to the 19th-20th Dynasties, i.e. from the
beginning of the thirteenth to the mid-twelfth cent. BC. Nine
other sites in the valley also produced the same Midianite
pottery. In the following deliberations we shall not deal with
the chronological aspects of each of the Timna' sites, but
discuss only the dating of the finds from the Timna' Sanctuary,
which constitute up to now the only stratigraphically secured
basis for the dating of the Midianite pottery.

2.3.1 Site No. 200 - The Egyptian Sanctuary: GR 1457 9090

Site No. 200, located next to the "Pillars of Solomon" -
a famous tourist attraction in the centre of the Timna' valley -
was discovered in 1966 by B. Rothenberg and several Midianite
sherds were found on its surface. Excavated in 1969, it turned
out to be an Egyptian mining sanctuary, dedicated to the goddess

Hathor. About 25% of the pottery found in the sanctuary was
Midianite and the homogeneity of its vessel types and the great
variety of their decorations were most remarkable. Most of the
vessels were large and small bowls, jugs and juglets, but there
was also a unique votive cup (Fig. 8). Outstanding were bird
drawings on juglets, mainly ostriches, and the drawing of a
human figure (Fig. 7). Representative samples of this pottery
were subjected to detailed petrographic examination and
identified as Midianite pottery, identical with the pottery
from Qurayyah (TS 1105-1107, 1136, 1206, 1207, 1212-1215).

The Midianite pottery from the Timna' Sanctuary was dated
on the basis of inscribed Egyptian votive objects of fayence
and glass, found in all layers of the Egyptian-Midianite
sanctuary. There were cartouches of Ramesses II, Merenptah,
Sethos II and Queen Twosre of the 19th Dynasty, and Ramasses
III-V of the 20th Dynasty, i.e. the Midianite pottery of this
sanctuary must be dated to the period from the beginning of the
13th cent. BC (c.1290 BC) to the middle of the 12th cent. BC
(c.1152 BC).

2.3.2 Camp No. 2: GR 1148 9107.

This site was excavated in 1964 and 1966 and Midianite
pottery was found in all of its layers - near the furnaces, in
the slag heaps and workshops - together with other pottery
groups: Negev ware and ordinary, wheel-made Egyptian and local
vessels. By analogy with the pottery from Site No. 200, the
pottery from Site No. 2 was dated to the 13th-12th cent. BC.
In the main there were large deep bowls, jugs and juglets and
goblets. Most were decorated with geometric designs, but there
were some large bowls with no decorations. A very large quantity
of Midianite pottery was found on a hilltop above the smelting
camp, which apparently served as a Midianite cult site
(Rothenberg, *Timna*, 112-117). Samples of all types of Midianite
pottery from Camp No. 2 were subjected to petrographic
examination by A. Slatkin, and there is no doubt that they all
belong to the Midianite group /35/.

2.3.3 Camp No. 30: GR 1447 9093

This site was excavated in 1974 and 1976. The same pottery
groups found at Camp No. 2 and Site No. 200 - Midianite, Negev
and ordinary Egyptian and locally made - were found in Layers
III-II, in the main representing production periods of Camp No.

30. There were also the same types of vessels: large bowls and
small delicate bowls with flat bases, bi-conical jugs and
juglets.   Most vessels show the typical Midianite decoration,
but there are some, mainly among the large bowls with flat bases,
that have a thick red and brown slip but no decoration.

The comparison of the Midianite pottery from Camp No. 30
with the pottery found in excavations and surveys of the other
Egyptian-Midianite sites of Timna', indicate a very close
resemblance, and there is no doubt that Camp No. 30 was in
operation at the same time as the Sanctuary and other Timna'
sites.   Petrographic examination showed the identity between
the pottery of Camp No. 30 and the Midianite pottery (Groups
A-B) from Qurayyah (TS 1059, 1060, 1061, 1062, 1101-1104).

2.3.4 Copper Smelting Camp No. 34: GR 1450 9090

Camp No. 34 (formerly Kh. Mene'iyeh), is the largest
smelting camp in the Timna' Valley.   It is located on top of
a hill which is strewn with large slag heaps.   At the time of
the 'Arabah Survey a considerable quantity of pottery was found
among the slag, some of it belonging to the Midianite group /36/.
There are not enough sherds with indicative shapes to determine
the type of Midianite vessels in use at the camp.

2.3.5 Site No. 3: GR 1452 9100

This site was mainly a residential camp, with dry built
houses of several rooms, and traces of metallurgical activities.
Among the pottery gathered around the houses was a large number
of Midianite sherds (Rothenberg, *Tsefunot Negev,* 31).

2.3.6 Work Camp No. 13: GR 1454 9107

During the 'Arabah Survey a large number of sherds were
collected at this site, but only one Midianite sherd: the rim of
a deep bowl with geometric designs inside and outside
(Rothenberg, *Tsefunot Negev,* 35-36).

2.3.7 Residential and Work Camp No. 14: GR 1452 9103

During the 'Arabah Survey a large quantity of pottery
including some Midianite sherds, among them a decorated juglet
handle, were found.   Material and decoration of the Midianite
sherds from this camp are identical with the Midianite sherds
from the other Timna' Valley sites (Rothenberg, *Tsefunot Negev,*
32-35).

2.3.8 Smelting Camp No. 15: GR 1456 9108

During the 'Arabah Survey many Midianite sherds were found
in this camp, both decorated and plain. There were sherds of
deep bowls, jugs and juglets. The Midianite pottery of Camp
No. 15 is identical in material, shape and decoration with the
pottery from Camps Nos. 2 and 30 (Rothenberg, *Tsefunot Negev*,
32-35).

2.3.9 Camp No. 185: GR 1459 9090

This camp was discovered in 1967 in the course of the Eloth
District Survey (B. Rothenberg, in Z. Ron (ed.), *Seker Khevel
Eloth* [The Eloth District Survey] (1967), 312). It was
primarily a work and residential camp, but there were also
traces of metallurgical activities. There were a number of
Midianite sherds among the pottery found at this site.

2.3.10 Site No. 419: GR 1452 9114

This site is located in a concealed ravine along the path
between Sites Nos. 15 and 2. It is almost completely destroyed,
but some debris of buildings are discernible and there are copper
smelting slags and other signs of copper production. Much
pottery, including a considerable number of Midianite sherds
of the kind found in the other Timna' sites, was found at
Site No. 419. (This site has not yet been published.)

2.3.11 Site No. 198: GR 145 909

This site is on top of the central massif of the Timna'
Valley (Har Timna'). Within a cave, formed by a huge boulder
that had fallen from a hilltop and remained leaning against a
rock face, stood a roughly dressed stone "stela" (Mazebah) on a
low stone "table". At its foot we found two vessels, one a
large "Negev" bowl, and the other a Midianite jug with a bi-chrome
geometric decoration on a yellowish slip (fig. 6:8) (Rothenberg,
Timna, 119, fig. 35, pl. 53).

2.3.12 Site No. 199: GR 145 909

Some fifty meters from Site No. 198 are enormous boulders
three to five meters high, at the bottom of which are a number
of niches. Some were intentionally blocked by stone slabs. The
niches were found empty but may have served as burial places
associated with the nearby "cave sanctuary" or "bamah" (Site No.

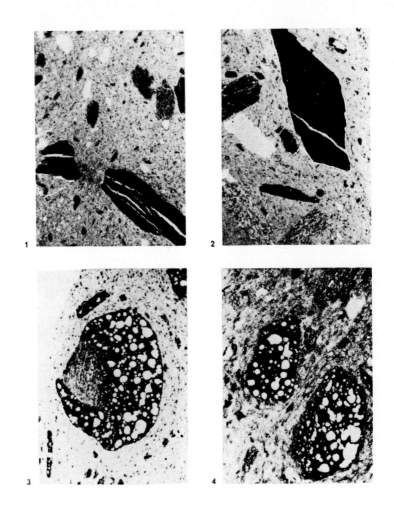

P1.I: Photomicrographs 1-4

1. Mag. X 30 - normal light   - Qurayyah   - TS n. 1134
2. Mag. X 30 - normal light   - Timna' Site 30- TS n. 1103
3. Mag. X 30 - normal light   - Kh. Duwâr   - TS n. 1128
4. Mag. X 30 - normal light   - Timna' Site 30- TS n. 1101

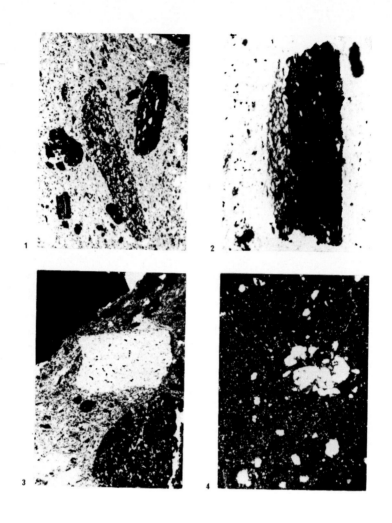

Pl.II: Photomicrographs 1-4

1. Mag. X 30 - normal light   - Qurayyah   - TS n. 1110
2. Mag. X 30 - normal light   - Tel Far'ah   - TS n. 1139
3. Mag. X 30 - normal light   - Timna' Site 30 - TS n. 1105
4. Mag. X 30 - polarized light - Qurayyah   - TS n. 1111

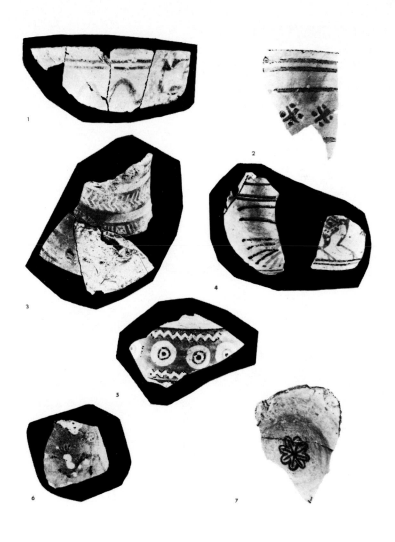

Pl.III: Midianite pottery from Timna' - T.2: 1,7; T200; 2-6

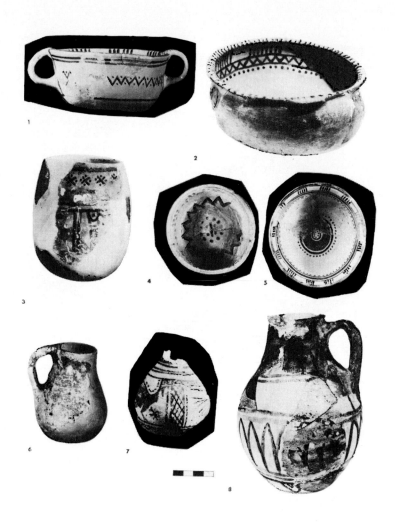

<u>PL.IV</u>: Midianite pottery from Timna' - T.2: 2-4,6,8; T200: 1,5,7; T.198:8

198). A number of sherds were found near the niches, among
them decorated Midianite sherds (Rothenberg, in Z. Ron (ed.),
Seker Khevel Eloth, 314; *id. Timna,* 118).

2.4 Western Palestine

Excavations in the Hebron hills and in South-Israel
uncovered isolated specimens of Midianite pottery.

2.4.1 Jedur: GR 1588 1156

Publications: S. Ben-Arieh, *Kadmoniyot,* 11 (1978); *id.
Eretz-Israel,* 15 (1981), 115-126.

Sarah Ben-Arieh /37/ excavated a tomb near the village of
Jedur, north of Hebron, which could be dated by the accompanying
burial gifts, including some imported Aegean objects, to the
Late Bronze Age, more precisely, from the late fourteenth to
the middle of the thirteenth cent. BC. Among the burial
offerings was a small Midianite bowl with geometric decorations.
Its petrographic examination proved it to be identical with the
Midianite pottery from Qurayyah and Timna' (TS 1099).

2.4.2 Tel Masos (Kh. el-Meshash): GR 146 069

Publications: V. Fritz, A. Kempinski, *ZDPV* 91 (1975), 116,
T.7B; *ibid.* (1976), 83-104; Y. Aharoni, V. Fritz, A. Kempinski,
Enc. of Arch. Excav. in the Holy Land, III (Tel Aviv, 1977),
816-818.

Eight sherds with geometric decorations in black and red
were found in the Tel Masos excavations. According to the
photography, they may be part of a single vessel. The
excavators identified these sherds as Midianite, dating them,
according to their archaeological context, to Iron Age I, i.e.
between mid-twelfth century and mid-eleventh century BC. One
sherd (TS 1170) was examined petrographically and identified as
Midianite in material and decorations.

2.4.3 Lachish (Tel ed-Duweir): GR 135 108

After the Tel Lachish excavations were resumed in 1973, a
number of decorated sherds were found and identified as
Midianite. These sherds have not yet been published and no
information is available on their archaeological context /38/.

2.4.4 Tel Far'ah (Tel Sharuhen): GR 100 076

Publications: J.L. Starkey, G.L. Harding, *Beth Pelet* II (1932), 29, pl. LXIII, 52-55.

The Tel Far'ah excavations of 1928-1929, directed by Petrie, uncovered a number of unusual decorated sherds first identified as Midianite by Dayton /39/. Of the three decorated Midianite sherds found by Dayton in the Institute of Archaeology, London, two were parts of a juglet with drawings of ostriches, similar to some found at Qurayyah (Parr *et al., ibid.*, fig. 15:9, 16:6) and at the Timna' Sanctuary (B. Rothenberg, *Timna*, pl. XXIV, fig. 47) /40/. According to the excavation report (*Beth Pelet,* 29) these sherds were found in a Philistine context. In the opinion of Olga Tufnell (reported by Dayton, *ibid.*, 28) they should be dated to 1220 BC.

The two sherds F367 and F364 (*Beth Pelet,* pl. LXII, 54155) were examined by the authors. Their decorations were made in three colours, black, red and brown on a yellowish background. One of the sherds was subjected to a petrographic test (TS 1137) and there is no doubt that the two belong to the Midianite pottery group.

An additional sherd (No. 37219, F/60, TS 1139) was found by one of the authors (B.R.) in the collection of the Institute of Archaeology in London. It is a large fragment of a jug with a creamy slip and geometric decoration in red and brown. This decoration too has its counterparts among the Timna' pottery (see e.g. *Timna,* pl. XXIII, 1). A complete Midianite juglet, with only traces of decorations, from tomb No. 542 at Tel Far'ah, was found in the collection of the Rockefeller Museum (PAM 4237) and examined petrographically (TS 1100). It seems that besides the above, more Midianite sherds were found at Tel Far'ah. Sherds 52 and 53 on Beth Pelet, pl. LXII and perhaps also No. 42, appear to us to belong to the Midianite group. E. Oren /41/ informed us that he found six or seven Midianite sherds from Tel Far'ah in the collection of the Institute of Archaeology in London, and according to his investigations they were found under the floor of the "Residency", i.e. they belong to the 13th-12th cent. BC and in his opinion antedate the three sherds mentioned above, which were found above the floor of the "Residency".

2.5 Sinai

The Sinai Survey of the "Arabah Expedition", conducted in
1967-1978 under the direction of B. Rothenberg, covered
considerable areas of northern and southern Sinai and recorded
more than three hundred sites /42/. Not a single Midianite
sherd was found there, not even in the Egyptian sites of the
19th-20th Dynasties. However, along the coastal strip,
connecting Egypt with Israel, Midianite sherds were discovered.

2.5.1 Bir el-'Abd: GR 9596 0497

Publications: E. Oren, *Kadmoniyot* 6 (1973), 101-103; *id., IEJ* 23
(1973), 112-113.

An Egyptian fort was found in excavations near the Bedouin
village of Bir el-'Abd. It was obviously erected there to
protect the Egyptian military road to southern Canaan. One of
the silos uncovered at the fortress, dated to the 19th-20th
Dynasties, contained three decorated sherds which the excavator
classified as Midianite.

2.6 Eastern Palestine (Jordan-Edom)

Glueck's publications are still a useful source of
information on Edomite pottery, although, as has recently become
evident, he did not distinguish between Edomite pottery of the
Late Iron Age and Midianite pottery of the New Kingdom /43/.
It is, however, rather difficult to determine the identity of
sherds from Glueck's illustrations and photographs. A collection
of the sherds from Glueck's surveys in Eastern Palestine, now in
the Rockefeller Museum in Jerusalem, was recently examined by
M. Weippert, A. Kempinski and one of the authors (B.R.) and a
small number of Midianite sherds were identified. These as well
as a number of typical Edomite sherds from Glueck's collection
and from C.-M. Bennett's excavations in Tawilan and Buseirah, in
southern Jordan, were subjected to petrographic tests, and an
essential difference between Edomite and Midianite pottery could
be defined in detail. As only a small part of the pottery from
Edom collected by Glueck is held in Jerusalem, the distribution
map of Midianite pottery in Jordan remains, so far, fragmentary
/44/.

2.6.1 <u>Tawilan</u>: GR 196 970

Publications: N. Glueck, *AASOR*, XV (1935), 82-83, 123-137, pl.
27A-B; *id.*, *BASOR*, 188 (1967), fig. 2, p. 13; Parr *et al.*,
op. cit. 8-9 (1970), 239; C.-M. Bennett, *Levant,* 3 (1971), V-VII.

Glueck noted especially the large number of decorated
"Edomite" sherds found in the survey of Tawilan (*AASOR*, 1935,
83). In his first publications, he dated the Tawilan sherds to
Iron Age I (*ibid.*, 83) but in 1967 he changed his mind. Comparing
the decorated sherds from Tawilan, Timna' and Tel el-Kheleifeh,
he decided they all belonged to Iron Age II. However, because
of the great similarity of the Edomite decoration from Tawilan
to those common in Palestine in the Late Bronze Age and in
Iron Age I, Glueck concluded that some of the Tawilan pottery
might belong to Iron Age I.

Of the published Tawilan pottery (*AASOR*, XV (1935), pl.
27A; *BASOR*, 188 (1967), fig. 2) only sherd No. 1 appears to us
to be Midianite, resembling the Timna' sherds, but all the rest
are similar to the Edomite sherds from C.-M. Bennett's excavations
examined by the authors. At the Tawilan excavations C.-M. Bennett
found only typical Edomite pottery of the 8th-6th cent. BC
(*Levant*, 3 (1971), VII), but during a survey of the region of
Tawilan, one Midianite sherd was discovered (P. Parr, *ibid.*,
239). This sherd was examined by the authors and found to be
identical with the Midianite sherds of groups A-B from Qurayyah
and similar ones from Timna' (TS 1177).

2.6.2 <u>Kh. esh-Shedeiyid</u>: GR 199 933

Publications: N. Glueck, *AASOR,* 15 (1935), 60-61, pl. 27A:2.

Glueck published only one sherd from Kh. esh-Shedeiyid, but
this is hard to identify from the photograph. In the
Rockefeller Museum we found one body sherd of a juglet of
creamy colour, from the same site, which upon petrographic
examination proved to belong to the Midianite group (TS 1127).

2.6.3 <u>Kh. Duwar</u>: GR 210 003

Sherds from this site, which has not been published /45/,
were found in Glueck's collection at the Rockefeller Museum.
One of them, a yellowish sherd from a bowl with red decoration,
was examined petrographically (TS 1128) and found to be Midianite.

2.6.4 <u>Amman</u>

Publications: J.B. Hennessy, *PEQ* 98 (1966), 155-162; P. Parr, *et al.*, *op. cit.*, 8-9 (1970), 239, n. 56.

In the area of the Amman airport, excavations uncovered a temple of the Late Bronze Age, dated by the excavators to the late fourteenth and the thirteenth cent. BC. According to a personal communication by J.B. Hennessy, the finds at Amman included several vessels of Midianite pottery /46/.

2.6.5 <u>Kh. en Nahâs</u>: GR 193 010

Publications: N. Glueck, *BASOR,* 55 (1934), 7-8; *id.*, *AASOR,* XV (1935), 26-30, 129-130, pl. 23, 27A.

Primarily a copper smelting site, it was surveyed in 1932 by Horsfield, Head and Kirkbright, who found there a sherd from a large decorated bowl with flat base (Glueck, *AASOR,* XV, 130). According to the description and photograph this sherd may be Midianite. Comparing it with a similar sherd from Timna', Glueck (*ibid.*, 130) dated it to Iron Age I. It is interesting to note that at Kh. en Nahâs Glueck himself found no "sherds of this delicate Edomite type" (Glueck, *ibid.*, 29), which the present authors believe to be later Edomite pottery.

2.7 <u>Unacceptable Identifications</u>

Various scholars have proposed to identify as Midianite certain sherds found during surveys of N.W. Arabia and in excavations in Western Palestine. We shall deal here with two such proposals because of the historical and archaeological importance of the two sites.

2.7.1 <u>Khuraybah</u>, near el-'Ula in the Hejaz.

Parr-Harding-Dayton reported a collection of sherds from Khuraybah, which included a considerable number with decorations resembling those of Midianite pottery (Parr *et al.*, 204-214 and drawings). The authors did not relate the Khuraybah pottery to the Midianite group from Qurayyah. Dayton (*Proc. Fifth Seminar* (1972), 25-26), defined the decorated ware from Khuraybah as Iron Age Edomite pottery. Additional sherds from Khuraybah were published by Winnett and Reed /47/ and one piece seemed to them to resemble the (Midianite) pottery of Tayma, though its ware appeared to them "Early Arabic" (*Ancient Records,*

177).   Comparing drawings of the Khuraybah pottery with the
published pottery from Timna', Qurayyah, etc., V. Fritz (*ZDPV* 91
(1975), 116) identified the same with the Midianite pottery
found in Tel Masos. We have examined a representative series
of sherds from Khuraybah from the Parr-Harding-Dayton collection
in London, and there is no doubt that the Khuraybah sherds do
not belong to the Midianite pottery groups.

2.7.2 Tel Ajjul

Publications: W.F. Petrie, *Ancient Gaza II* (London, 1932), 12,
pl. XLI: 42.

In Petrie's excavations a jug was found in tomb 1099,
decorated with geometric motifs somewhat resembling those on
the Midianite pottery found at Qurayyah and Timna'. In the
Parr-Harding-Dayton report (*ibid.*, 239) and Dayton's article
(*ibid.*, 28) it was identified as Midianite pottery. We examined
the vessel, now in the Rockefeller Museum (No. 32-1942),and did
not find the features characteristic of all types of Midianite
pottery. It is a bi-conical jug, made of very chalky material
without any visible temper, and apparently belongs to the
"Chocolate on White" group /48/ antedating the pottery of Timna'
as well as groups A and B from Qurayyah.

3.   The Midianite Pottery of Timna' /49/

We publish here a number of drawings of Midianite pottery
from Sites Nos. 200 (the Sanctuary), 2, 30 and 198, representative
for the repertory of the Midianite pottery from Timna', relating
to shape as well as decoration. We shall not here compare
individual vessels or particular decorations with those of other
pottery groups in the region, and this for two reasons: (i)
The Timna' Midianite pottery is basically "foreign" to the
region; (ii) The dating of the Midianite pottery of Timna' is
based on well-dated Egyptian inscriptions, found in the same
archaeological context as the Midianite pottery, and not on
typological comparisons.

We shall also not deal with the important problem of the
cultural connections and the "genetic" origins of the Midianite
pottery, but try and establish the direct physical provenance of
the Midianite pottery found at Timna' and other places in the
region. In our opinion all the Midianite pieces came from
Qurayyah in N.W. Arabia, and/or a site close by.

3.1 Typology

3.1.1 Bowls (fig. 3; 4:2; 5:1-4)

Found in a range of sizes, small, medium and large, with
the same characteristics: flat bases, almost vertical sides and
decorations inside and outside.

3.1.2 Jugs (fig. 5:5-9; 6:6-9)

The diameter of the flat base is smaller than that of the
body. There is one handle, connecting the body with the neck
(fig. 6:8-9). Almost all jugs are decorated on the outside.

3.1.3 Juglets (fig. 6:1-4)

These vessels have a piriform body and a flat base. The
handle goes from the body to the cylindrical neck. Sometimes
the inner diameter of the neck tapers towards its base.
Geometrical motifs containing drawings of a bird (see fig.
7:2-5) are the typical decoration of the juglets.

3.1.4 Goblets (fig. 4:1, 3)

These vessels have a high straight wall, wide open mouth
and a flat base. They are decorated on the outside but also
slipped inside.

3.1.5 Varia

3.1.5.1 Cup (fig. 8) with mouth and base of equal diameter and
concave body. From both the base and rim, platform-like
protrusions are connected by a double handle. Only the outside
of this vessel is decorated.

3.1.5.2 Large, possibly krater-shaped vessels (fig. 7:1-2) with
thick walls, decorated only at the outside.

3.2 The decorations

All the decorations appear to be hand-painted, but the
bands running around the vessel may have been applied with the
aid of a slow wheel. All vessels are slipped with a thick
layer of cream slip and were often also burnished. The
decorations are usually in darker colours - tints of black,
brown and red-brown - than the colour of the slip.

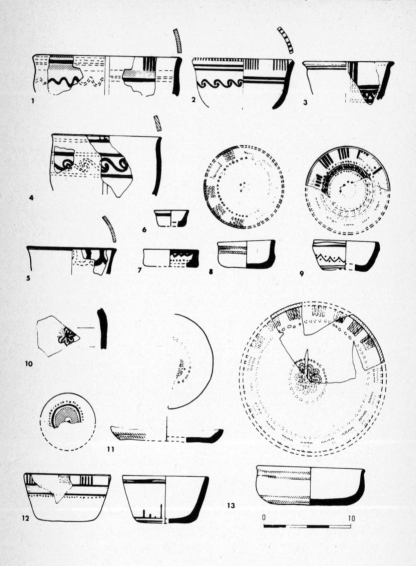

Fig.3
1-13 bowls (Site No.200)

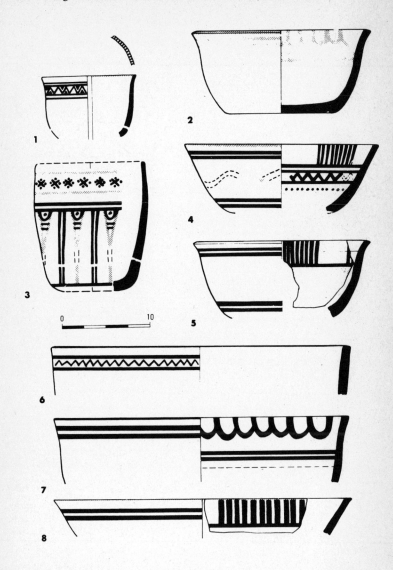

Fig.4
1, 3 goblets; 2, 4-8 bowls (Site No.2)

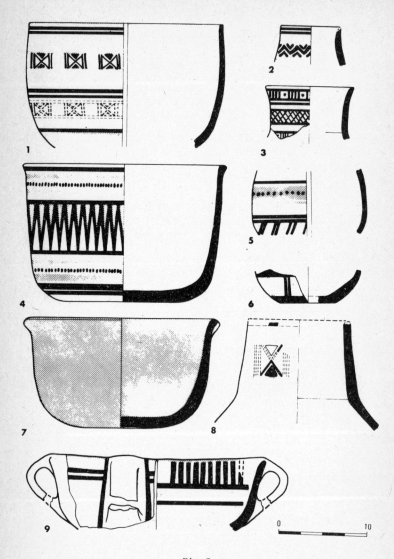

Fig.5
1-4, bowls (Site No.2); 5-9, jugs (5, 8, 9, Site No. 200; 6,
Site No. 2)

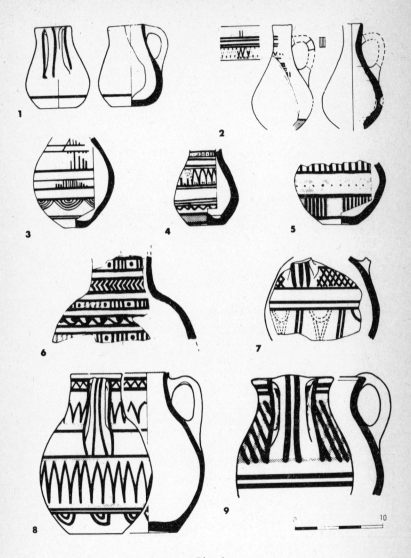

Fig.6
1-4, juglets (1, Site No.2; 2-4, Site No. 200);
5-9, jugs (5, 7, 9, Site No.2; 6, Site No. 30; 8, Site 198)

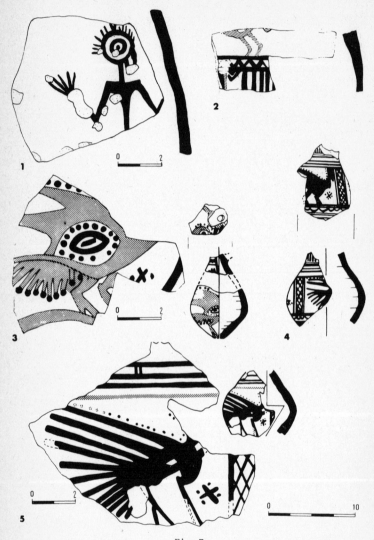

Fig.7
1, human figure; 2, krater (?) with bird drawing; 3-5, juglets
with bird drawings (all from Site No. 200)

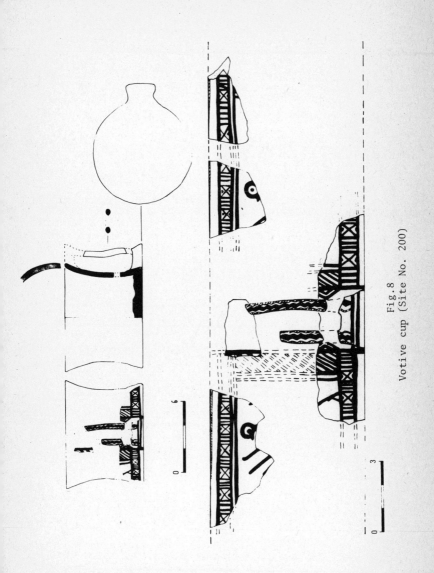

Fig.8
Votive cup (Site No. 200)

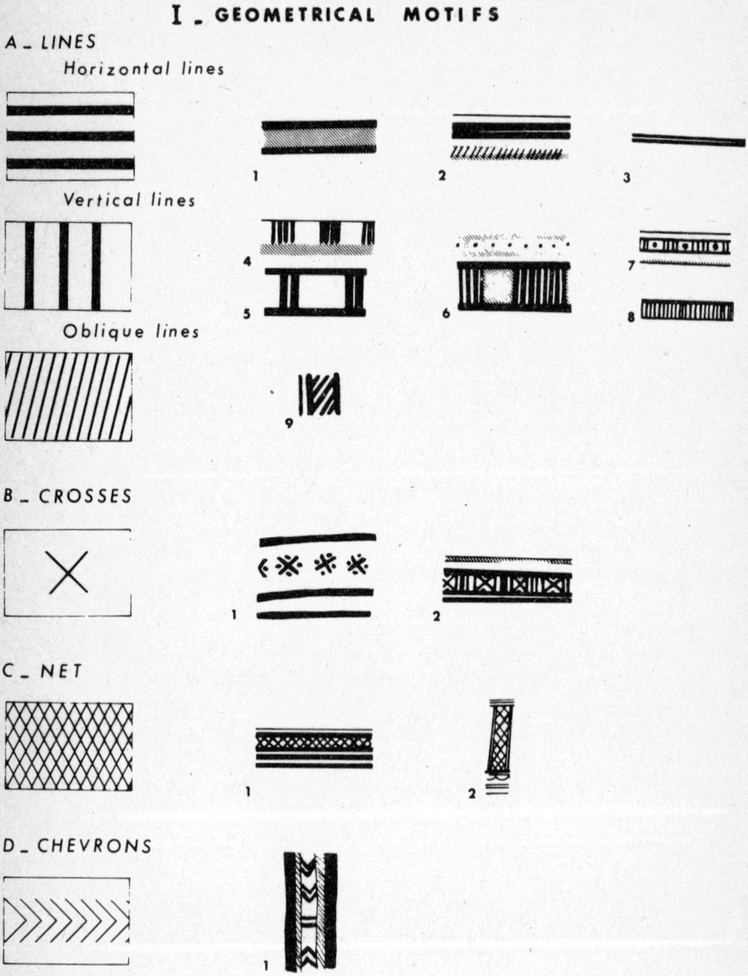
I - GEOMETRICAL MOTIFS
A - LINES
Horizontal lines
1
2
3
Vertical lines
4
5
6
7
8
Oblique lines
9
B - CROSSES
1
2
C - NET
1
2
D - CHEVRONS
1

Fig.9
Midianite motifs

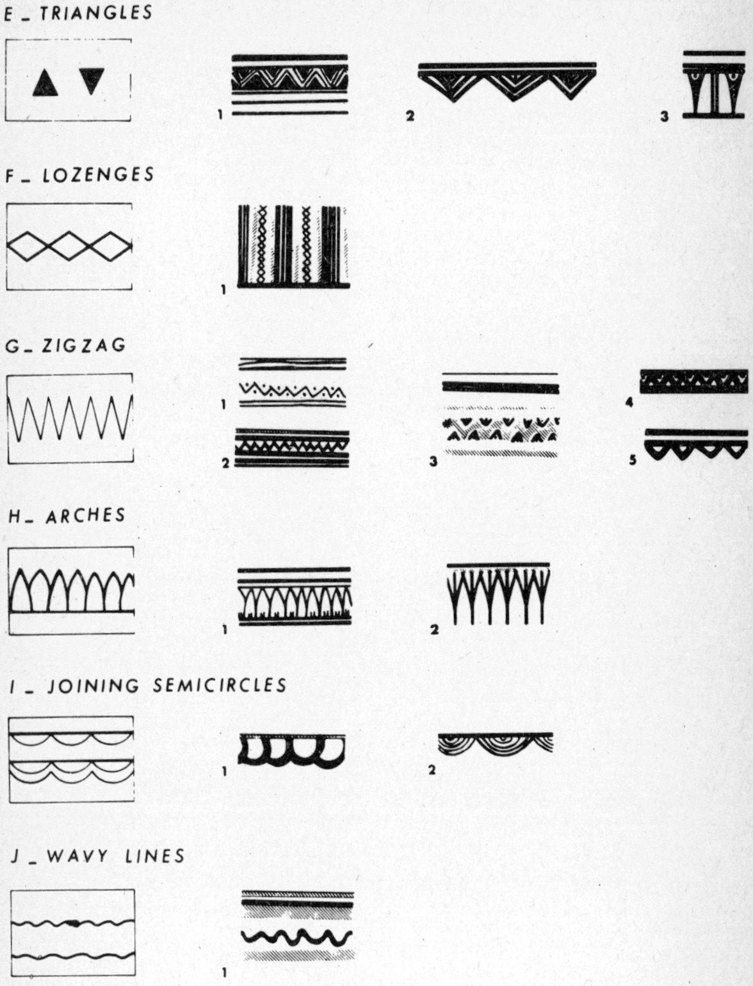

E _ TRIANGLES

F _ LOZENGES

G _ ZIGZAG

H _ ARCHES

I _ JOINING SEMICIRCLES

J _ WAVY LINES

Fig.10
Midianite motifs

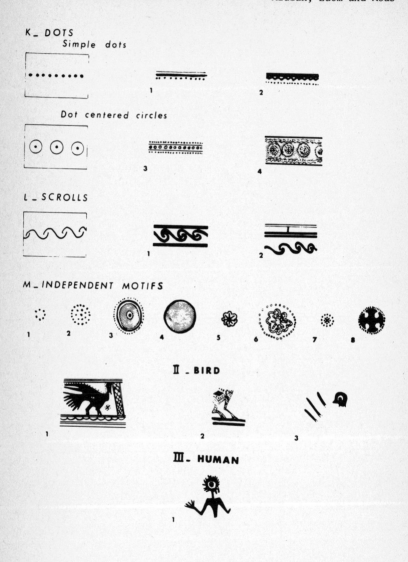

Fig.11
Midianite motifs

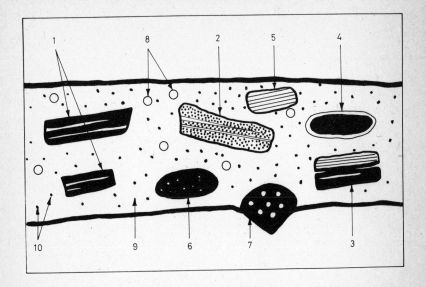

Fig. 12

Schematic section of a Midianite sherd, showing all the
characteristic elements of Midianite pottery that can be
identified with an unaided eye or with the aid of a
simple magnifying glass.

1. Black shale fragments broken into sub-plates.
2. A red shale fragment broken into sub-plates.
3. Banded shale fragment with a black broken band and
    a lighter silty band.
4. A black shale fragment separated from the body by
    a continuous peripheral cavity.
5. A light shale fragment with a platy structure.
6. A partially melted shale fragment with rounded edges
    and spherical cavities (gas bubbles).
7. A partially melted shale fragment that lost its
    rectangular form, became mobile and penetrated through
    the sherd's surface. It has large spherical cavities
    (gas bubbles).
8. Rounded quartz grains.
9. The light groundmass.
10. Iron-oxide-rich concretions in the groundmass.

Relation between type of vessel and decorated surfaces:

	Bowls	Jugs	Juglets	Goblets	Varia
Outside and inside	+				
Outside only	+	+	+	+	+
Inside only	+				

Among the small bowls we find decorations applied inside or outside but also both together. All other pottery types have decorations only at the outside surface.

There are three major categories of decorative motifs: geometrics, birds and a human figure /50/.

3.2.1 Geometric

Geometric motifs are the most common of the Midianite pottery decorations. They can be divided into thirteen basic motifs which appear together in various combinations. Each of these combinations has a dominating motif with others serving as frame or fill.

Fig. 9-11 list the motifs in order of increasing complexity. Each motif, indicated by a capital letter, is characterised by a schematic drawing (in a frame at the left) and then shown as it actually appears on the pottery.

A - parallel lines, including:
      horizontal lines   (fig. 9:A 1-3)
      vertical lines   (fig. 9:A 4-8)
      oblique lines   (fig. 9:A 9)
B - crosses   (fig. 9:B 1-2)
C - nets   (fig. 9:C 1-2)
D - chevrons   (fig. 9:D 1)
E - triangles   (fig. 10:E 1-3)
F - lozenges   (fig. 10:F 1)
G - zigzag   (fig. 10:G 1-5)
H - arches   (fig. 10:H 1-2)
I - joining semicircles (fig. 10:I 1-2)
J - wavy lines   (fig. 10:J 1)
K - dots and dot-centred circles (fig. 11:K 1-4)
L - scrolls   (fig. 11:L 1-2)
M - independent motifs (fig. 11:M 1-8)

3.2.2 Birds

Birds, apparently ostriches, were depicted quite
realistically, though somewhat formalised, with some variations
in detail. They have long, bent legs and cleft claws (fig.
7:3-5); a long neck and a head sometimes drawn as a dark circle
with a dot in the centre (fig. 11: M3). The body is painted
solid, but often with an "eye" of a dotted circle in the middle.
There are long and spread wings and a shorter tail, mostly
fanning out from one point.

3.2.2 Human figure

A strange human figure was drawn in black on a lighter
background (fig. 7:1). It shows a schematic representation of
a head, rather reminiscent of the bird's head on fig. 9 /51/.

3.2.4 Additional observations on types and decorations

All types of decorated vessels show geometric motifs, but
bowls, goblets and jugs have only geometric decorations.
Although the decorations differ from vessel to vessel, some
common features can be distinguished:

1. The geometric motifs are arranged as a frieze around the
    inside and/or outside of the bowls.

2. All the bowls show a red or brown band on the rim.

3. Small bowls show an "independent motif" of Group M
    (fig. 11: M 1-8) on the inside of its flat base.

4. All vessels have two parallel lines, below the rim, on
    the outside. All vessels which show a central motif on
    their outside have two additional parallel lines near
    the base.

5. The jugs have normally several geometric friezes, one
    above the other, whilst the other vessels show only one
    frieze. These friezes are also more elaborate and crowded.

6. The bird motif, contained in a frame of geometric metopes,
    is characteristic for the juglets (fig. 7), though there
    are juglets that bear only geometric decorations (fig. 6:1-4).

3.3 The Midianite pottery of Timna' - like all Midianite pottery
wherever found - is rather limited from the point of view of
vessel types. The shapes are on the whole very primitive and

the wheel used - if at all - must have been very slow. Some
of the shapes are strongly reminiscent of the primitive hand-
made "Negev" ware, which was found at Timna' (apparently not at
Qurayyah) in the same archaeological context.

There is a remarkable contrast between the primitive shapes
and paucity of types of the Midianite pottery, and the
sophisticated and variegated decorations on most of its
vessels. These include complicated and delicate geometric
designs in several colours and in various combinations hardly
ever repeated, painted with a brush on a slipped and often
carefully smoothed and burnished surface, while in regard to
shape these vessels are quite primitive and sometimes even
irregular and mis-shapen. Despite the primitive shapes,
however, most of the Midianite pottery can be described as
handsome and sometimes even artistic.

At the smelting sites excavated at Timna' (Sites Nos. 2
and 3), most of the pottery found consisted of large bowls -
some undecorated - and jugs. These were mainly "domestic"
vessels, and no large Midianite vessels for storage or transport
were found. It is obvious that the metal workers at the Timna'
camps used the decorated vessels for their daily use and did not
consider them as anything special. On the other hand, at the
"bamah" (high place) F of Site No. 2 /52/ and in the Egyptian-
Midianite Sanctuary (Site No. 200), the majority of the vessels
were small, delicately-shaped with particularly intricate
decorations. Evidently these vessels and of course the special
votive cup were brought to the Timna' Sanctuary as offerings to
Hathor.

3.4   Dating the Midianite pottery of Timna'

Midianite pottery was found at twelve sites in the Timna'
Valley, but only three of them were excavated. The date of the
use of this pottery at Site No. 200 - the Hathor Sanctuary -
could be fixed by Egyptian inscriptions and inscribed objects,
found in the same sealed layers, to the period from Ramesses II
to Ramesses V, i.e. from c.1290 BC to c.1152 BC. All the
pottery from Site No. 200 was meticulously compared with the
pottery found in the excavations of Sites No. 2 and 30 and their
basic conformity became evident. This result relates not only
to the Midianite pottery, but also to the "Negev" ware and to
the imported Egyptian and locally manufactured "normal",
wheel-made pottery. As in the Sanctuary, where Midianite sherds

were found on the floors of all the New Kingdom layers, so at
Sites No. 2 and 30 the Midianite pottery appeared in all layers,
dated - by comparisons with the material at the Sanctuary - to
the 13th-12th cent. BC.

Further comparison of the pottery collected during our
surveys in the Timna' Valley at Sites Nos. 34, 3, 13, 14, 15,
185, 198, 199, which are still unexcavated, with the stratified
pottery finds from Sites Nos. 200, 2 and 30, showed great
homogeneity of all pottery groups. We do of course, not
automatically assume that consequently all the sites listed
above had the same span of life.

On the contrary, we have good archaeological reasons to
assume that e.g. Site No. 2 was established some time after
the building of the Hathor Sanctuary (Site No. 200) and that
the beginning of activities at Site No. 30 perhaps antedates
the building of the Sanctuary. Nevertheless, the period from
Ramesses II to Ramesses V must be considered the chronological
frame of the New Kingdom sites of Timna' and consequently - at
this stage of our research - we date the Midianite pottery of
Timna' to the period from the beginning of the 13th cent. BC to
the middle of the 12th cent. BC.

4. The provenance and technology of the Midianite pottery -
   a petrographic synthesis

The overall archaeological picture that emerged from the
study of the properties and distribution of the Midianite
pottery raises several questions:

Are the materials used in the manufacture of all Midianite
vessels (so far investigated) indeed identical, as they appear
to be to the unaided eye? What are the dominant characteristics
shared by the material of all these vessels? How do these
vessels differ from each other in their material properties?
Can these differences be correlated with other pottery attributes
and/or with possible sites of provenance? What are the main
technological characteristics of Midianite pottery? Would it
be possible to prove the assumption that the Midianite pottery
originated in Qurayyah, in N.W. Arabia /53/?

A satisfactory answer to these questions requires objective
analytical tools. From the range of analytical procedures that
are commonly used in pottery studies we have chosen the

petrographic analysis because of its suitability to examine a
wide range of pottery problems, including those of provenance
and technology. Petrographic analysis is based on microscopic
examination of polished thin sections that are interpreted in
the light of mineralogical, ceramological, and geological
concepts. Petrographic data makes possible (a) a detailed
comparison of ceramic materials in terms of their mineralogical-
petrographic composition and texture, (b) a consideration of
the geological province in which the pottery was manufactured,
(c) an evaluation of the technological knowhow of the ancient
potter in choosing and preparing his materials, (d) an enquiry
into the effect of firing on the materials and an evaluation of
firing conditions.

   This article is based on the microscopic observation of 35
polished thin sections and binocular observations of about a
hundred sherds. The polished thin sections represent Midianite
pottery from Qurayyah (nine samples), the Timna' Sanctuary (ten
samples), Timna' Site No. 30 (eight samples), three sites in
Jordan (Edom) (Tawilan, Kh. Duwar and Kh. esh-Shedeiyid (one
sample from each), Jedur in the Hebron mountains (one sample),
Tel Masos in the Beersheba region (one sample) and Tel Far'ah
(three samples).

4.1 General description

   Systematic examinations of Midianite pottery from the
various excavations and surveys indicated its great homogeneity
in properties such as hardness, fracture, surface characteristics,
texture, the nature of non-plastic ingredients and colours.
Clear correlations between pottery attributes such as function,
shape, size and decoration on the one hand and the properties
of the basic material are not yet apparent. While they may
emerge from a more detailed study, they are not likely to
modify the overall picture and the main conclusions of this
report. Small, delicate, thin-walled vessels resemble large,
coarse, thick-walled vessels in their general material
appearance, although there is a slight tendency to lighter
colours in the ceramic body of the smaller vessels.

   This general description is based on observations by the
unaided eye and a magnifying glass. These observations do not
require any special analytical skill and they are presented here
separated from the microscopic observation so as to provide
archaeologists with a tool for a preliminary comparison of

Midianite pottery that may be uncovered in future excavations.

4.1.1 Colour. In a fresh broken fracture the sherd body
occurs in light colours including milky white, cream white,
greyish white, light pink and light red. In these light
colours, Midianite pottery differs from the majority of ancient
pottery types manufactured in the Levant, as most of the clay
deposits available for potters in this region are relatively
iron-rich, and thus fire to darker colours.

The colours vary from sample to sample. In some sherds
the greyish colour dominates, indicating a reducing atmosphere
at least during the final stages of firing. Colour zoning is
also very common, and the most pronounced differences appear
between body (section) and surface colours, due to a special
treatment of the surface, including slipping, burnishing and
painting.

4.1.2 Hardness. Midianite pottery is commonly very hard
compared to other contemporaneous ceramic materials. This
property, together with the light colours, makes Midianite
pottery resemble modern stoneware.

4.1.3 Shale fragments. Black and red fragments are easily
observed in a freshly broken fracture. These are a very
characteristic feature of Midianite pottery and they are clearly
visible, especially due to pronounced colour contrast with the
light ground mass (fig. 12). These fragments occur in various
quantities and shapes in the different samples examined. In
thin-walled vessels the fragments are usually smaller and occupy
a smaller total volume, and they increase in proportional
quantity and size in larger thick-walled vessels.

The colour of these fragments differs from sample to
sample. In sherds in which the body is light-grey the fragments
are predominantly black or very dark brown, while in sherds in
which the body colour ranges between milky white, cream white
and light pinkish, the fragments are predominantly red /54/. In
quite a few samples, both red and black fragments occur.

Most fragments exhibit a rectangular section. Observing
their section parallel and normal to the sherd's surface
reveals that the fragments are plates of more or less equal
dimensions parallel to the platy surface. These bodies exhibit
occasionally a splitting into secondary subplates (fig. 12:1,2,4).

Both the rectangular section and the secondary splitting suggest that these fragments are derived from hard shaley rocks and not from crushed pottery (grog) /55/. Only extremely thin-walled pottery could be expected to break into rectangular forms of the dimensions exhibited by the fragments of Midianite pottery, but even these would not possess an internal structure that might explain the secondary splitting parallel to the plate boundaries.

The transition from red to black shale fragments is commonly associated with the rounding of their edges. In the most extreme examples of this transition the fragments were modified into completely spherical shapes. This transition is sometimes accompanied by the progressive development of tiny spherical voids in the rounded black fragment. In their general appearance these tiny voids resemble occurrences of gas bubbles in viscous materials such as volcanic rocks, slag, etc. It is therefore assumed that these fragments have undergone partial melting during firing and behaved like viscous materials changing to spherical bodies. In some very extreme and uncommon cases among the samples examined here, the partially molten fragments became so mobile that they managed to protrude through the outer surface of the sherd (fig. 12:6,7). In addition to the dark fragments, there are in some samples light fragments which appear to the unaided eye in creamy milky white tones (see Pl, I, 1-4; II, 1). Due to their light colour, these fragments are not as easily distinguished except where the body is relatively dark. In shape and size the light fragments resemble the dark ones. In most samples the darker fragments are more numerous, sometimes very much more, and only in a few cases is the opposite true.

4.1.4 Quartz grains. With the aid of a magnifying glass or binoculars one observes that in addition to the shale fragments there is always some sand temper. Sand grains are well rounded and almost exclusively composed of quartz.

4.1.5 Surface properties

4.1.5.1 Turning marks. Inner sherd surfaces frequently exhibit wide ridges and much finer striations parallel to them. These marks resemble so-called "wheel marks". However, the general impression is that the turning speed was not very high and so it appears that the wheels used were not of a very advanced nature. Also the general shape of almost all Midianite

vessels deviates from what fast turning movement can be
expected to produce. On outer surfaces, these turning marks
were obliterated or totally wiped away by various treatments
applied to this surface (smoothing, slipping, burnishing).

4.1.5.2 <u>Smoothing and slipping of the outer surface</u>. Most
outer surfaces of the Midianite pottery are covered with a
creamy white slip. The slip probably served several purposes,
but mainly provided a background of uniform colour for the
painted designs. The slip covered the dark shale fragments that
give the surface a coarse spotty texture, not suitable for the
fine painted designs.

4.1.5.3 <u>Painting</u>. The detailed examination of some painted
sherds indicated that a wide range of colours was used,
including light yellowish-brown, red, dark-brown and black
and all shades between. The lighter tones usually occur as a
very thin layer, sometimes even semi-transparent. The darker
colours occur as thicker layers and their tones resemble the
range of colours exhibited by the shale fragments. Colour
variability differs from sample to sample. In many vessels
there are three or even more distinct colours. On vessels where
different coloured strips cross each other, it is possible to
determine the order of application of the colours. As a rule
the lighter colours were applied first and the darker ones
later. In some cases it was possible to determine three stages:
the first light yellowish-brown, the second red and the third
black.

4.1.5.4 <u>Melting phenomenon</u>. Some of the dark coloured surfaces
are characterised by a glassy appearance. Black glassy surfaces
are sometimes accompanied by a fine net-like texture of tiny
ridges. These surfaces apparently represent a selective partial
melting of material relatively rich in iron oxide that acted as
a flux, thus reducing the melting point. In a few cases also
lighter surfaces exhibit the development of a glassy phase. In
these cases a transparent layer of glaze with tiny spherical
voids was formed. The melting of the light surfaces indicates
relatively high temperature.

4.2 <u>Microscopic analysis</u>

Detailed microscopic analyses of various mineralogical and
textural attributes of the Midianite pottery revealed a
homogeneous picture; there is no way by which the sherds from

I. Opaque, iron-oxide rich argillaceous shales	II. Opaque and dark iron-oxide-rich silty shales	III. Dark, platy, argillaceous silts	IV. Various light quartzo-feldspathic silts
V. Light shales spotted with tiny iron oxide concretions	VI. Light silty shales spotted with tiny iron-oxide concretions	VII. Light platy, argillaceous silts	
VIII. Light argillaceous shales	IX. Light silty shales		

Table I

the various sites could be distinguished from each other.
Although it is possible to define characteristic properties
of this or that sherd, there is no grouping of such
characteristics according to the sites. In fact, individual
pottery samples from different sites may resemble each other
more closely than samples from the same site. As will be shown
later, all the differences between the samples can easily be
explained by the heterogeneous nature of one and the same
varigated shale formation and there is no need to postulate
several sites of origin for the Midianite pottery. It became
evident that the Midianite pottery was manufactured in one
workshop or in a group of workshops close to each other, using
one and the same shale deposit as the major source of raw
material. The description of the microscopic examination of
the thirty five polished thin sections from the various sites
is therefore treated as a single unit.

4.2.1 Shale Fragments

4.2.1.1 Petrographic classification. The petrographic analysis
shows that the shale fragments are quite varied in composition
and texture. To illustrate their range of properties the shales
were classified schematically as shown in Table 1 overleaf.

    Two major variables determine the microscopic variance
among the shale fragments:

(a) The content of the quartzo-feldspathic silt fraction /56/.
In Table No. 1 the content of this fraction increases from left
to right along the horizontal axis. On the left side of the
table are the pure argillaceous shales without any silty
nonplastics. These change gradually along the axis to silty
shales, to platy argillaceous silts, and lastly, on the right
of the table, to quartzo-feldspathic silts without any clay
minerals.

(b) The intensity of the red colour, which indicates semi-
quantitatively the iron oxide content. This increases along
the vertical axis from top to bottom. The boundaries between
the shale types in this table are based on microscopic
observations and do not represent absolute quantities.

    The microscopic analysis reveals a gradual transition
between the various shale fragment types. However, some of the
types are more common than others. The opaque argillaceous
shales (type 1) for instance, are very common and in some sherds

they are the dominant type, while some of the other types occur
only as isolated fragments. In other sherds one may find a
great variety of shale types, representing almost the whole
range of the table: opaque, dark, light, argillaceous and silty
in almost equal proportions (Pl. I, 1, 3).

In most samples the opaque and dark fragments (types I and
II:Pl. I, 1, 2) dominate and only in a few samples the light
fragments belong to more than one type. In that case the
different types occur in thin layers parallel to the platy
structure and the elongated form of the fragment. In most of
these layered fragments we find types which belong to a
horizontal line in Table 1, i.e. the layers differ from each
other in the content of the silty fraction (Pl. II, 2). The
layered shale fragments indicate a close physical association
of the various shale types in their natural environment. The
range of shales and silts observed as nonplastic fragments in
the Midianite pottery represent, therefore, a variegated, very
finely layered and laminated, shale formation that is
characterised by alternations of various shales, silty shales
and silts.

4.2.1.2 Behaviour of the shale fragments during the forming
        of the vessels

During the forming of the vessels the shale fragments,
including the argillaceous types (types I, V and VIII), behaved
like rigid particles. This is evidenced by the preservation of
the rectangular form, the platy structure and the perfectly
parallel orientation of their platy minerals. Shale fragments
have been observed in many other types of pottery from the
Levant, but as a rule they are not perfectly rigid, their
original platy shape is deformed into lenticular forms, and
their inner structure is distorted.

The rigid nature of the shale fragments in the Midianite
pottery suggests that the original shale deposit was more than
usually lithified and that in order to prepare a plastic and
workable paste, it had to be mechanically broken down and wetted
for a long period. Alternatively, their unusual rigidity could
be explained by prefiring before the fragments were added to
the plastic paste as nonplastics. The use of shale fragments
as a predominant nonplastic ingredient is a deviation from the
usual techniques of pottery making. This phenomenon can perhaps
be explained by the absence of alternative suitable nonplastics
in the geological environments in which this pottery was

manufactured. The absence of other coarse nonplastics, aside
from the quartz sand even in minor quantities, strongly
indicates that such nonplastics were indeed lacking geologically
in the area close to the pottery workshops.

4.2.1.3 Modification of the shale fragments during drying and firing

Microscopic observations suggest that after the vessels
were formed, the shale fragments underwent several modifications.
The argillaceous fragments and among these mainly the iron oxide
rich types (Type I) exhibit two features connected with
shrinkage (decreased volume) relative to the sherd body of
the fragments. Fragments with a well-developed platy structure
exhibit a splitting into subplates and an opening of tabular
cavities between the subplates (Pl. I. 1); others, with less
developed platy structure, tend to shrink more homogeneously
towards their centre, leading to the development of a peripheral
cavity (Pl. I. 2). This process led in extreme cases to the
complete detachment of the fragment from its surroundings. It
is difficult to decide whether this shrinkage occurs during
drying due to loss of absorbed water and/or during firing due
to sintering processes. The greater degree of shrinkage of
the shale fragments, in comparison to the body, can be explained
by the proportionally lower volume of quartzo-feldspathic silt.

A more pronounced modification of the fragments is the
loss of their original rectangular shape and the complete
metamorphosis of their inner structure. These fragments tend
to take on rounded shapes and gradually lose their inner platy
structure until they become a dark, black, homogeneous
isotropic and structureless material. This is accompanied by
the development of tiny spherical cavities (Pl. I, 3, 4; II, 1).
These phenomena occur mainly in fragments of Types I and II, and
can be explained by a partial melting of the fragments. The
onset of partial melting is manifested by the occurrence of
greenish band-like areas that gradually spread over the entire
fragment, accompanied by the first spherical cavities. At this
early stage of partial melting the cavities are small, not
perfectly spherical, and occupy a relatively small volume. At
this stage the fragment has not yet completely lost its
rectangular shape. As melting progresses, the cavities increase
in size, become perfectly spherical and the fragments change in
shape beyond recognition. These spherical cavities are gas
bubbles, and have the effect of volume increase which balances,

and sometimes even exceeds, the volume decrease due to the shrinkage of the solid particles. The overall increase in the volume of the partially molten fragments is reflected in the absence of peripheral shrinkage cavities and by the development of concentric structures in the body surrounding the molten fragments. These indicate the force exerted by the swelling of the fragments in their more refractory surroundings.

The most pronounced melting of shale fragments is discernible in sherds which are mainly greyish in colour, suggesting reducing conditions. The peripheral shrinkage cavities and the concentric structures surrounding molten shale fragments must be due to modifications caused by the firing of the vessel. A prefiring stage of the fragments would not account for such phenomena. This conclusion, however, does not exclude the possibility that shale fragments were prefired at a low temperature.

4.2.2 Other nonplastics. In almost all of the thirty-five polished thin sections a small volume proportion of quartz is present and occurs as individual single grains and in a few cases as small aggregate of sandstone. These quartz particles are about ten times larger than the silty quartz that is an original component of the light shales from which the plastic past was prepared.

4.2.3 Composition of the body. The sherd body is identical in composition and texture to the light shale fragments (Types IX, VII, VI and V) and differs from them only in the loss of the parallel arrangements of platy minerals, so characteristic of the shale fragments. The sherd body in most cases is composed of light silty shales (Type IX), sometimes of spotted silty shales (Type VI) and less often of argillaceous shales (Types V and VIII). Midianite pottery was never made of iron-oxide-rich red shales (Types I and II). It is not certain if the choice of Types IX, VII, VI and V for the body and the restriction of the use of the red types as nonplastics is due to differences in properties connected to the cold working stage (difference in plasticity, shrinkage during drying) or to differences in behaviour during firing. There is no doubt that the Midianite potters were fully aware of the refractory quality of the light shales, especially under reducing condition, as they must have noticed the lower melting point of the iron-oxide-rich shale fragments, and the tendency of dark painted surfaces to become glassy.

5. The Provenance of Midianite Pottery

From the petrographic analysis it becomes evident that the
Midianite pottery originated from a single centre of
production. The question of location of this central workshop
will be examined here by comparing the geological environment
of the various sites where Midianite pottery was found with the
geological environment of the production centre deduced on the
basis of the petrographic analysis. Petrographic studies of
ancient pottery have shown that in areas where a large and
variegated part of the geological section is exposed the
various components of this section will be present in the
pottery. This principle is valid mainly in relation to coarse-
grained pottery with abundant nonplastics reaching and exceeding
2 mm in diameter. The geological environment of the Midianite
pottery workshop, indicated by the petrographic analysis, is
governed by one family of rock types: variegated shales (iron-
oxide-rich, iron-oxide-poor, silty and argillaceous), quartz-
feldspathic argillaceous silts, pure silts and quartz-rich
sandstones. Common to this family of rock is the total absence
of carbonate-bearing lithologies. Such a lithological complex
agrees best with the paleozoic Nubian sandstone complex that is
composed mainly of quartz-rich sandstones with intercalations
of silty and shaly lithologies.

Among the sites under consideration here, Qurayyah is the
only one that is located in a purely Nubian sandstone terrain.
Detailed geological information on Qurayyah and its surroundings
is not available, but we can refer to a geological section from
the area of Tabuk, published by A.H. Helal /57/, which is most
relevant to Qurayyah (about 70 km north of Tabuk). In the
upper part of this section, which includes the lower part of
the paleozoic Nubian complex, we find a formation of shales and
sandy silt about a hundred metres thick. Qurayyah and Tabuk are
part of a platform where the geological formation is almost
undisturbed, and therefore the same part of the geological
section is exposed over extensive areas. Such an extensive
areal distribution of lithologies fits in well with the
homogeneous petrography of the Midianite pottery.

Further support for this conclusion comes from Parr's
description of the Qurayyah hill as being composed of "grey
green silt stone". The top of this elongated hill is divided
into three parts by two walls built of "thin, flat slabs of
local siltstone set in mud." In Parr's photographs the stone

slabs that were used as building material exhibit a very
pronounced splitting into fine plates. As far as one can tell
from the photographs, these stone slabs are derived from
argillaceous sandstones, argillaceous silts, or even shales.
The well-developed platiness of these building stones could
very well represent a megascopic reflection of the banded
micro-structure that was observed in the shale fragments of
the Midianite pottery.

We may now conclude that the views formulated by
B. Rothenberg in 1972 about a N.W. Arabian provenance of the
Midianite pottery /58/ could now be verified by geological
evidence.

To properly round off this discussion we must also examine
the geological environment of the other sites where Midianite
pottery was found. In Timna', where large quantities of
Midianite pottery were found, a paleozoic Nubian sandstone
complex is exposed only as part of a thick geological section,
including a variety of igneous rocks (in the heart of the Timna'
Valley), a wide range of calcareous lithologies and a variety
of clay-rich formations with abundant carbonate components.
This section provides a great number of alternative raw materials
for pottery making - nonplastic as well as clay-rich plastic
materials. These materials figure abundantly in other types
of pottery found and probably made at Timna', but never in the
Midianite pottery. If Midianite pottery was also made in
Timna', there should be a way of distinguishing it from the
Qurayyah ware, but according to the results of our petrographic
analysis, no such distinction can be made. The logical
conclusion is that no Midianite pottery was manufactured in
Timna'. This does of course not exclude the possibility that
potters of Midianite origin worked in Timna' and produced other
wares.

The Edomite sites where Midianite pottery was found are
situated geologically above the Nubian section. Kh. esh-Shedeiyid
is located at the edge of Senonian rock exposures, Tawilan is
located just above the Nubian sandstone formations, in an area
which includes a variety of carbonate rocks, and Kh. Duwar is
in a similar geological environment and close to wide exposures
of volcanic rocks. Again, as in the case of Timna', the
geological nature of the environments of these three Edomite
sites is not reflected in the Midianite pottery found there.
On the other hand, the samples of the Midianite pottery from

these sites closely resemble the samples from Qurayyah. The
rest of the sites in Israel and Sinai are completely outside
the Nubian province, in areas in which carbonate rock, hard
rocks, as well as clay-rich lithologies predominate. Three of
these sites - Jedur, Tel Masos and Tel Far'ah - were examined
petrographically and their geological environments are not in
agreement with the petrography of Midianite pottery. We may
now conclude that, by the evidence obtained so far, the
Midianite pottery originated in a workshop or in a number of
workshops in Qurayyah and its surroundings.

6.   Summary and Conclusions

6.1 Petrographically there is no difference between the
Midianite pottery from the various sites examined, in spite of
the great distance between them and the extreme differences in
their geological environments. This leads to the conclusion
that all the pottery examined originated in one or several
pottery workshops in the same neighbourhood, using the same
geological deposit.

6.2 All the materials needed for making Midianite pottery were
obtained from the same geological formation of variegated
carbonate-free shales. Light silty and argillaceous shales
were used to prepare the plastic paste, while dark-red, iron-
oxide-rich shales were used as nonplastic temper. This
functional differentiation is sharp and there is not even one
sample of Midianite pottery where the body was made of a dark
shale material. Slips and paints quite probably also came from
the same shale formation.

6.3 The basic materials of which all the Midianite pottery was
made differ from the materials of most ancient pottery groups
of the Near East, mainly by the total absence of carbonates.
The raw material of the Midianite pottery consists of refractory
mixtures that are similar to those of the stoneware of the
modern potter. The use of such refractory materials in the
making of Midianite pottery is primarily a reflection of local
geological conditions and cannot be ascribed to any known
tradition of ceramic technology.

6.4 The use of shale fragments as temper is also a characteristic
feature of the Midianite pottery. This is also due to the
uniform local geology, i.e. the absence of other coarse
nonplastics (the quartz sand that was used as a secondary

nonplastic is finer than the shale fragment). However, a
technological explanation for this feature cannot altogether
be excluded. Ferruginous shales were selectively chosen as
nonplastics. While there is no completely satisfactory
explanation for this choice, the unusual behaviour of these
shales during firing suggests that they were favoured because
of their less refractory nature. Whether or not the shale
fragments were prefired remains an open question.

6.5 The geology, reflected by the petrography of the thirty-
five samples, is homogeneous and agrees with the local geological
condition near Qurayyah. The three Edomite sites (Kh. esh-
Shedeiyid, Kh. Duwar and Tawilan) and the Israel sites (Timna',
Tel Masos and Jedur) are all located in geological environments
that contradict the petrography of the Midianite pottery.
These basic facts lead to the only possible conclusion that all
Midianite pottery was manufactured at or near Qurayyah.

6.6 Petrographically and typologically, Midianite pottery,
regardless of where it was found outside N.W. Arabia - Israel,
Sinai, Edom, Timna', or the 'Arabah - belongs to groups A and
B of Qurayyah, with the exception of a few isolated sherds of
groups E and F also found in the Timna' Sanctuary. This fact
is particularly important because groups A, B, E and F are
dated at Timna' by Egyptian inscriptions to the 13th-12th
cent. BC. On the other hand, other ceramic groups found at
Qurayyah undoubtedly belong to other, perhaps also later,
periods. This latter pottery is, however, made of the same
raw material typical for the Qurayyah pottery and must also
be of local manufacture. We must therefore assume that
Qurayyah was the production centre of Midianite pottery from
which it spread through commercial channels or by the movement
of people whose base was Qurayyah.

6.7 Because of the lack of archaeological information on the
Hejaz, it is still impossible to determine whether Midianite
pottery was produced exclusively at Qurayyah. There may have
been other centres in the Hejaz, such as Tayma, located in the
same geological environment as Qurayyah.

6.8 On the basis of the Timna' Sanctuary, the Midianite pottery
of the A, B, E and F groups is dated to the 13th-12th cent. BC.
The fact that only sherds of these groups have been found widely
distributed outside the Qurayyah - as far as the Hebron hills
and northern Sinai - points to unique historical processes during

the 19th-20th Dynasties, not as yet investigated.   The
distribution of Midianite pottery during this period may have
been closely bound up with Egyptian control of the region.
Furthermore, since many Midianite sherds have been found in
copper smelting camps in the Arabah, and Midian itself must
be considered an ancient mining centre, where gold, silver and
copper ore deposits were exploited in ancient periods on a large
scale /59/, the wide distribution of Midianite pottery could
well be connected with metal production and trade.

6.9   At all sites where Midianite sherds were found, they
belonged to the 13th-12th cent. BC horizon.   It may therefore
be assumed that groups A and B of the Qurayyah pottery were in
use mainly during that period, which lasted about 150 years.

6.10 It should be noted that only very few Midianite storage
or transport vessels were found in Timna', except for a small
number of jugs and juglets.   Most of the vessels found are
"kitchen and tableware" of various types.   Similar to the
cooking pots of the period throughout the whole region even
the typical cooking pot at Timna' was locally hand-made Negev
ware rather than Midianite or "ordinary" wheel-made pots.
Large storage vessels and those designed for transport, i.e.
most of the pottery in the Timna' camps, belong to groups of
"ordinary" wheel-made pottery, either made in Egypt or locally
manufactured.   The apparent function of the Midianite pottery
at Timna' indicates that it was imported by people who came
there from Arabia - probably skilled and experienced
metallurgists - and who used these vessels for their daily
requirements in the smelting camps, or as gifts to Hathor at
the Egyptian-Midianite mining sanctuary.   The classification of
the Timna' pottery according to their functions presents an
instructive picture of the logistic set-up of a copper industry
in the desert, and of the ethnic composition of the miners and
metal workers as well as of their "landlords".   In that picture
the Midianite pottery is a crucial factor.

6.11 Our distribution map of the Midianite pottery reflects the
spread of Midianite vessels over a considerable area, but it
should be borne in mind that it is based on only partial surveys
and isolated excavations.   The fact that Midianite pottery has
only recently been identified as a group in its own right
probably accounts for its scarcity in excavation reports.   Yet
it is the Midianite pottery - because of its unique features that
make it possible to identify its provenance with certainty -

which can provide a reliable chronological criterion (at least
as regards the groups dated by the Timna' Sanctuary), and
evidence for connections with the Arabian peninsula.

7. Photomicrographs

Pl. I.1   Dark and opaque shale fragments (types I and
             II). The opaque fragments exhibit elongated
             tabular shrinkage cavities, breaking the
             fragments into subplates. The dark fragments
             do not exhibit shrinkage phenomena, due to a
             higher proportion of a quartzo-feldspathic silt
             fraction. The opaque fragments are almost
             silt-free.

Pl. I.2   Dark and opaque shale fragments (types I and
             II). The large opaque fragments show peripheral
             shrinkage cavities. In fragments of types II
             and III there are no indications of differential
             shrinkage. The small dark particles either
             represent tiny shale fragments or iron-oxide
             concretions which are original components of the
             light shales of type VI (which in this sample
             form the body).

Pl. I.3   Partially melted shale fragments. In the large
             fragment there is still an unmelted remnant in
             which the fine platy structure is still preserved.
             Its rounded shape is secondary and connected with
             the softening accompanying partial melting. Around
             this fragment the body shows a weak concentric
             alignment of platy particles, due to forces caused
             by the volume increase in the fragment. Partial
             melting in this sample was probably facilitated
             by a reducing atmosphere during firing.

Pl. I.4.   Partially melted shale fragments.

Pl. II.1.   Various types of shale fragments in a spotted
             shale body of type VIII. In the opaque fragment
             showing a few spherical cavities partial melting
             is in its early stage. The rectangular shape is
             still preserved, but the platy texture has been
             obliterated. Due to a more refractory composition,
             the other fragments do not show any signs of partial
             melting.

Pl. II.2   Dark banded shale fragment composed of two bands:
            the right band is almost opaque (argillaceous and
            iron-oxide-rich) and the left band is silty. The·
            banded fragments indicate an intimate association
            of various shales in the geological outcrop.

Pl. II.3   Three common types of shale fragments. The
            fragment in the upper left corner is type I (opaque
            argillaceous and ferruginous shales). The fragment
            at the centre is type VII (platy, light argillaceous
            silts), and the fragment at the bottom right is
            type II (dark, ferruginous silty shales). The
            body is darker than the light fragment in the centre
            of the photograph and belongs to type VI (light
            silty shales spotted with tiny iron-oxide
            concretions).

Pl. II.4   Various occurrences of the mineral quartz. The
            large illuminated grain in the centre is a fragment
            of sandstone, composed of more or less rounded
            quartz grains. The medium size bright grains are
            also quartz, derived from the sandstones; the tiny
            bright grains are also quartz, but these represent
            part of the silty fraction of the shale.

NOTES

/1/   B. Rothenberg, *Ha'aretz Museum Annual*, 12 (1970), 20;
P. Parr, G.L. Harding, J.F. Dayton, *Bull. Inst. of Arch.*, 8-9
(1970), 240.
/2/   A detailed discussion of the Timna' pottery, including
the Midianite pottery, will be published in B. Rothenberg, *et al.*,
The Mining Sanctuary of Timna' (forthcoming).
/3/   Jezirat Fara'un, now called "Coral Island", was first
examined by B. Rothenberg in 1957, when decorated sherds were
found. Only in 1960 were they identified as belonging to the
same group of sherds found at Timna'. See B. Rothenberg,
Tsefunot Negev (Tel Aviv, 1967), 211-212; *id.*, *God's Wilderness*
(London, 1961), 91.
/4/   N. Glueck, *AASOR*, XV (1935), 124-137.
/5/   B. Rothenberg, *PEQ*, 94 (1962), pl. XII: 1-6; Y. Aharoni,
ibid., 66-67.
/6/   Y. Aharoni, *ibid.*, 66-67.
/7/   Y. Aharoni, "ha-Keramika me-Atar No. 2 be-Timna"
(unpublished study). See also: N. Avigad, in *Eilat* (Jerusalem,

1963), 24; Y. Yadin, in A. Malamed (ed.), *Be-Yemei Bayit Rishon* (Jerusalem, 1961), 109. In the first report on the discovery of the ancient mines of Timna' (B. Rothenberg, *ILN,* 3 Sept. 1960, 383-385), the author dated the mines to the 11th-10th centuries BC.

/8/   B. Rothenberg and A. Lupu, *Ha'aretz Museum Annual,* 7 (1965), 14-21; 9 (1967), 51-63; B. Rothenberg, *RB,* LXXIV (1967), 80-85, pl. XII; *id., Timna'*(London, 1972), 67-111, 114-117.

/9/   B. Rothenberg and A. Lupu, *Ha'aretz Museum Annual,* 9 (1967), 62; B. Rothenberg, *Tsefunot Negev* (Tel Aviv, 1967), 27-28.

/10/   A. Lupu and B. Rothenberg, *Archaeologia Austriaca,* 47 (1970), 105. In the course of the investigation of the material from Timna' Site No. 2, especially from the second season of 1966, it became evident that the decorated pottery, together with the other groups found in the same layers, should be dated earlier than the 12th-11th centuries BC previously proposed. This new date was mainly supported by other pottery finds, mainly cooking pots, kraters, jars, pithoi, jugs and juglets, oil lamps, flasks and pyxis (see also B. Rothenberg, *Timna'* [London, 1972], 106-111, pl. 42-54).

/11/   Y. Aharoni, *PEQ,* 94 (1962), 66. Aharoni studied the pottery uncovered at Timna' Site No. 2 and first established the new date for the Timna' sites.

/12/   N. Glueck, *AASOR,* XV (1935), pl. 27A, 28A, 28B; *id., BASOR,* 188 (1967), figs. 1, 2, 4, 5.

/13/   B. Rothenberg and A. Lupu, *Ha'aretz Museum Annual,* 9 (1967), 62; *Tsefunot Negev* (Tel Aviv, 1967), 28.

/14/   B. Rothenberg, *ILN,* Arch. 2323 (15 Nov. 1969), 31-32; Arch. 2324 (29 Nov. 1969), 28-29; *id., Ha'aretz Museum Annual,* 12 (1970), 20-25; *id., Timna'* (1972), chap. V; *id., The Mining Sanctuary of Timna',* forthcoming.

/15/   The first petrographic tests were made by A. Slatkin (Haifa Technion). See B. Rothenberg, *Timna'* (1972), 162-163.

/16/   The reading of the Egyptian inscriptions was first entrusted to R. Giveon, who ascribed several of them to Seti I, as quoted in the preliminary report on the excavation (B. Rothenberg, *Timna'* (1972), 163). The Egyptian objects and inscriptions were eventually investigated by A. Schulman, according to whose reading the list of Egyptian kings in the Timna' Sanctuary begins with Ramesses II rather than Seti I.

/17/   The authors are most grateful to P. Parr and J. Dayton for their generosity in regard to the Hejaz finds and for their permission to conduct petrographic tests.

/18/ B. Rothenberg, *ILN,* Arch. 2323 (15 Nov. 1969), 32; *id.,*
Bible et Terre Sainte, 139 (1970), 6; *id., Midianite Timna'*
(London, 1971), 12, 15-23, pl. 34-35; *id., Timna'* (1972), 70-71;
P. Parr, G.L. Harding, J.E. Dayton, *Bull. Inst. of Arch.,* 8-9
(1970), 240; J.E. Dayton, *Proc. Fifth Sem. for Arabian Studies*
(London, 1972), 25-33, pl. I-IV.

/19/ The authors hereby extend their sincere thanks to
excavators and institutions that put sherds at their disposal
for petrographic examinations, and to the Stiftung Volkswagenwerk,
whose generous support made this research project possible.

/20/ Parr's dating was based on the general similarity of the
decorations from Qurayyah to those of the Late Bronze Age in
the ancient Near East, but especially on the pottery from the
Timna' Sanctuary. See P. Parr *et al., ibid.,* 239.

/21/ This pottery collection is now in the possession of Mr.
J.E. Dayton and we extend our thanks for his courtesy in
enabling us to review the entire collection again after the
first petrographic examination.

/22/ Sherds nos. 84, 4 and 8 in the Winnett-Reed report do not
appear to belong to the Midianite group. Sherd no. 4 is more
like the later sherds from Khuraybah.

/23/ This has lately been confirmed by M.L. Ingraham who
presented at the Colloquium on the History of Archaeology of
Late Bronze and Iron Age and N.W. Arabia (Institute of
Archaeology, London University, 3-4 April 1981) a series of
undoubtedly Midianite sherds from Tayma. Among these sherds
was one decorated with the drawing of a camel.

/24/ See below TS 1059. This sherd from Timna' Site No. 30
(T-30/76-439-4) is part of a large vessel, apparently a bowl
with straight sides. It is 14 mm thick, slipped and burnished
but not decorated.

/25/ After the Mesad Gozal excavations by Y. Aharoni in 1964,
the decorated sherds were handed over to him. Some time later
they were sent to Tubingen to M. Weippert, who was writing a
thesis on Edom, and went astray on their way back. Weippert has
examined them and attributed them to Hejaz pottery. See
M. Weippert's unpublished doctoral dissertation, *Edom,* n. 1407.

/26/ Meshel arrived at this date with some due hesitation
(Meshel, *Hadashot Arkeologiyot,* 96 (1975), 51). Methodologically,
caution is of course necessary in dating a site on the basis of
Midianite pottery alone. Although the Midianite pottery of
the Timna' Sanctuary could be absolutely dated, on the basis of
inscribed Egyptian finds, to the period between Ramesses II and
Ramesses V, this does not necessarily mean that the
chronological range of its use was everywhere the same as in

the Timna' Sanctuary. Meshel also stated that the vessels at
the Yotvata fortress "differ from those common in Judah and
found in the latest excavations in Edom", but are also not
identical with the pottery groups in Timna' *(Hadashot Arkeologiyot*
94-95 (1975), 34-35). We have examined the pottery from the
Yotvata fortress, now exhibited in the District Museum next
to Kibbutz Yotvata, and there is no doubt that it belongs to
the pottery corpus of 13th-12th cent. BC Timna'.

/27/ Meshel described this sherd as "a large fragment of a
krater of Midianite type decorated in red and black", but in
fact it appears to belong to a type of straight-walled flat-
bottomed deep bowls which is most common in the Midianite
repertory (see below).

/28/ See detailed bibliography, N. Glueck, *BA*, XXVIII (1965),
72, n. 2.

/29/ G.E. Wright, *BA* 22/4 (1959), 104 fig. 16a.

/30/ In his first publications (see *AASOR*, XV (1935), 137)
Glueck dated the "Edomite" pottery "from the beginning of EI, I
down to about the middle of EI, II, that is, from the first part
of the thirteenth century down into the eighth century BC".
Glueck's 1967 article thus embodied a drastic modification in
his dating of the "Edomite" pottery. Glueck apparently did not
recognise the fundamental difference between Edomite and
Midianite pottery and in the published plates both groups
appear mixed together. Since the Edomite pottery appeared in
Tel el-Kheleifeh as well as at Umm el-Biyara (C.-M. Bennett,
Antiquity, XLI (1967), 197) in a context of the 8th-6th cent.
BC, failure to distinguish between the Midianite and Edomite
pottery led to the ascription of such a late date to Midianite
pottery as well.

/31/ This jug was found by M. Kadishman and handed over to the
Israel Department of Antiquities, Jerusalem. Unfortunately it
could not be located in the Department's stores and was therefore
not examined by us.

/32/ See C.-M. Bennett, *Levant,* 5 (1973), 1, for a summary on
the dating of Edomite pottery; for plates of Edomite pottery
from Buseirah, see C.-M. Bennett, *Levant* 6 (1974), 19-24; 7
(1975), 8-15. We have conducted petrographic tests on a
considerable number of sherds from Buseirah and there is no
doubt that the Edomite pottery is fundamentally different from
the Midianite.

/33/ A similar conclusion was arrived at regarding the pottery
from Tel el-Kheleifeh by Z. Meshel (*Eretz Israel,* 12 (1975), 50)
who concluded that Glueck must have erred in relating the sherds
in question to stratum IV. It should be mentioned in this

connection that Y. Aharoni, in 1966, examined the finds from
Tel el-Kheleifeh in Glueck's institution in Cincinnati. He
noted that a number of decorated sherds resembling those from
Timna' were indeed found at Tel el-Kheleifeh, but *outside* of
Glueck's excavations. Because of the important implications
of the possible presence of 13th-12th cent. pottery in the
Tel el-Kheleifeh area, it would be important to re-examine all
finds and excavation records from the site. See B. Rothenberg,
Tsefunot Negev (1967), 284 n. 88.

/34/ Actually no evidence has yet been published for the
presence at Tel el-Kheleifeh of the kings of Israel or Judah;
see B. Rothenberg, *Tsefunot Negev* (1967), 200-202.

/35/ A. Slatkin conducted a number of tests on Midianite
pottery within the framework of a petrographic project related
to ancient pottery from Israel (see A. Slatkin, *Ha'aretz
Museum Annual,* 15-16 (1973), 101-111).

/36/ Camp No. 34, now called "Hill of the slaves", has long
been a tourist attraction and very few sherds remained on the
surface. Systematic excavations of this site are planned for
the near future.

/37/ We are grateful to Ms Ben-Arieh for making the pottery
available to us for petrographic examination and for providing
information on her excavation before its publication in 1981.

/38/ Unfortunately, the authors were not permitted to examine
these sherds from Lachish, though during a temporary absence of
Mr A. Ussishkin, director of the Lachish excavations, their
identification as Midianite was confirmed to us by Mr Barkai,
a member of the Lachish excavation team.

/39/ J.E. Dayton (*Proc. Fifth Sem. for Arabian Studies* (1972),
28). We were able to locate only two of those sherds, nos.
54-55.

/40/ Cf. fig. 1, a Midianite juglet with ostrich drawings, now
in the collection of the Nehushtan Pavilion, Ha'aretz Museum,
Tel Aviv (no. 1001). This vessel was acquired from a Jerusalem
antiquities dealer, and its provenance is purportedly Southern
Jordan.

/41/ Our thanks to Dr E. Oren of Ben-Gurion University, Beer
Sheba, for his great help in gathering information on the
Midianite pottery finds from Tel Far'ah and other sites. As
these lines are being written, efforts continue to locate the
sherds from Tel Far'ah that have not yet been examined by us.

/42/ B. Rothenberg, *P.E.Q.,* 102 (1970), 4-29; *id., Ha'aretz
Museum Annual,* 14 (1972), 31-45; 15-16 (1974), 16-34; *id.,
Sinai* (Bern, 1980).

/43/ See a comprehensive discussion of the problem in the dissertation of M. Weippert, *Edom* (Tubingen, 1971), 401-407. See also N. Glueck, *BASOR*, 188 (1967), 13, and also J.E. Dayton, *Proc. Fifth Sem. for Arabian Studies,* (1972), 25; P. Parr *et al., Bull. Inst. of Arch.,* 8-9 (1970), 239.

/44/ S. Mittmann has recently conducted further surveys in Jordan, but the pottery collected has not yet been published. See S. Mittmann, *Beiträge zur Siedlungs- und Territorialgeschichte des nördlichen Ostjordanlandes* (Wiesbaden, 1970).

/45/ Kh. Duwar appears on Map No. IIIb of N. Glueck (*AASOR,* XV (1935), but is not mentioned in the text of his report.

/46/ See further finds of Midianite pottery in C.-M. Bennett's excavations at the Amman Citadel: J. Kalsbeck, G. London, *BASOR,* 232 (1978), 47.

/47/ F.N. Winnett, W.C. Reed, *Ancient Records from North Arabia* (Toronto, 1970), 176-178, pl. 84.

/48/ See R. Amiran, *Ancient Pottery of the Holy Land* (Jerusalem, 1963), 158-159, pl. 49.

/49/ The authors thank I. Ordentlich and I. Mozel for their important contribution to the typology of the Timna' pottery. A. Hason prepared the plates of drawings, J. Gavish the distribution map.

/50/ In the Hejaz at least one additional motif was found - the camel (see above note 23). This is of course of considerable interest, because a large quantity of camel bones was uncovered in the 13th-12th cent. BC sites of Timna' (see forthcoming report by H. Lernau in B. Rothenberg, *The Mining Sanctuary of Timna',* forthcoming).

/51/ A similar, though in detail quite different, schematic drawing of a strange human figure was found in Qurayyah (Parr *et al., ibid.,* I, fig. 16).

/52/ See B. Rothenberg, *Timna'* (1972), 114-117.

/53/ See already B. Rothenberg, *Timna',* 182.

/54/ The atmosphere that prevailed in the kilns of the Midianite potters was quite variable. When oxidising atmosphere predominated, the ferruginous shale fragments became deep-red and the matrix cream-white to slightly reddish white. When a reducing atmosphere predominated, the ferruginous shale fragments became black and the matrix light-grey.

/55/ Crushed pottery (grog) is characterised by an irregular internal structure that is the result of mechanical disintegration of the original structure of the shale. This takes place during the preparation of the clay.

/56/ The silty quartzo-feldspathic fraction relates to tiny grains of quartz and feldspar, ranging in size between 2-64 microns.

/57/   See A.H. Helal, *Zeitschrift d. Deutsche Geolog. Gesell.*
117 (1956), 506-543.
/58/   B. Rothenberg, *Timna'* (1972), 182.
/59/   R.J. Roberts, *et al.*, *Mineral Deposits in Western Saudi
Arabia* (Jiddah, 1975).

List of Thin-Sections and Sites

TS	Field No.		Remarks
Site 30	1059		Original sample
	1066		Re-fired to 900°
	1061	439/4	Re-fired to 1100°
	1062		Re-fired to 1200°
	1101	943/35	
	1102	45/35	
	1103	228/1	
	1104	642/7	
Site 200 (Sanctuary)	1105	306/5	
	1106	306/4	
	1107	306/2	
	1206	306/1	
	1207	306/3	
	1212	234/146	
	1213	71/9	
	1214	287/31	
	1215	295/206	
	1136	258/21	
Qurayyah	1108	309/7	
	1109	309/5	
	1110	309/4	
	1111	309/3	
	1112	309/2	
	1113	309/1	
	1134		
	1211	309/6	
	1138	971	
Tawilan	1077	307/8	
		.69 .79	
Kh. Duwar	1128	.67	
Kh. esh-Sheideiyid	1127	254	

TS	Field No.		Remarks
Jedur	1099		
Tel Far'ah	1100	-542	
	1137	-367(64)	
	1138	/60. 37219	
Tel Masos	1170		

A LABORATORY RECONSTRUCTION OF LATE BRONZE-EARLY IRON AGE COPPER SMELTING IN THE ARABAH

John F. Merkel
Institute for Archaeo-Metallurgical Studies
Institute of Archaeology
University of London
31-34 Gordon Square
London WC1H OPY

At Timna Site 2, the remains of three large copper smelting furnaces with slag-tapping capabilities were excavated by Professor B. Rothenberg. The site was dated to the period of Egyptian New Kingdom exploitation of the copper deposits during the thirteenth to twelfth centuries BC. As a continuation of the post-excavation analysis, attempts were made to operate successfully a furnace simulation in order to reproduce the ancient metallurgical products under known conditions. This brief progress report presents a segment of the experimental program conducted by the author with the support of the Institute for Archaeo-Metallurgical Studies.

A shaft furnace was constructed of firebrick in the laboratory to better measure and control some of the major variables. It was an enhanced design of the large, Type A, furnace first used by Boydell in 1978. The dimensions were 32 cm internal diameter with a height of about 60 cm (figure 1). It operated with three inclined tuyeres, each delivering 350 liters of air per minute. About 75 kg of charcoal were consumed during a typical experiment. Twenty-two simulation experiments were conducted with this furnace type.

Large circular tapped slags are representative of the Late Bronze-Early Iron Age technology at Site 2, so this has been the emphasis of the experiments. Multiple taps cannot duplicate the structure of the ancient slag specimens. The largest slag circle produced as a single tap from the furnace has been 21.2 kg, which is approximately 2/3 the desired weight. The smelted copper associated with this experiment occurred as small, isolated ingots on the furnace bottom under each tuyere.

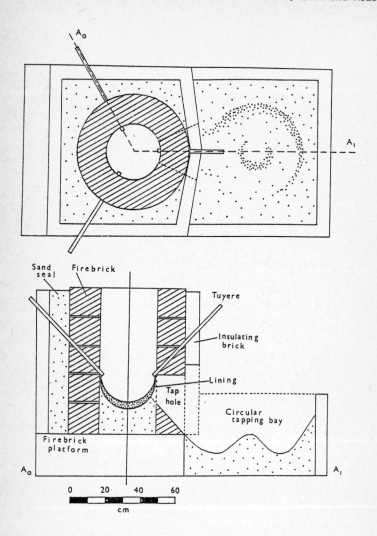

Figure 1.
Firebrick furnace simulation, showing section A_0-A_1.

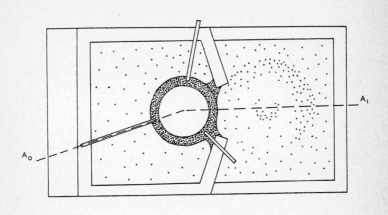

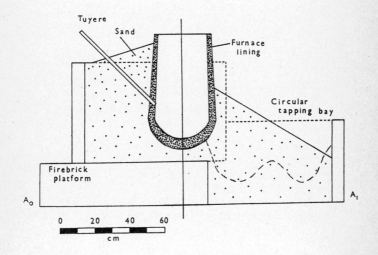

Figure 2.
Proposed reconstruction for Furnace IV at Timna Site 2.

Based on these experiments with the furnace simulation, a new reconstruction is proposed for Furnace IV at Site 2. Instead of firebrick, the reconstruction was built simply from coiled furnace lining into a sand pit. It had three inclined tuyeres and essentially the same dimensions (figure 2). Using generally the same operating procedure, the size of the circular tapped slag was increased to 25.9 kg. The separation of copper and slag was excellent. About half of the input copper ran out with the tapped slag, leaving a single plano-convex ingot weighing 2.2 kg on the furnace bottom.

Some questions still remain concerning the physical and chemical characteristics of the smelted copper. Only with the experimental reconstruction was a large tapped slag produced with a satisfactory plano-convex copper ingot. The average iron content of the smelted copper varied around 10%. The observed minor and trace element composition was expected on the basis of previous experience with the Timna copper ore (Tylecote et al., 1977). The possibility now arises that the plano-convex ingots of "pure" copper, known from the Late Bronze and Iron Ages, are refined products, rather than the primary result of smelting by direct reduction. Analyses of the copper-based objects from Timna Temple and Site 2 also show relatively high iron contents (Craddock, 1980). In an electric furnace, repeated melting of the high-iron copper from the smelting experiments did not readily decrease the level. Related work is in progress on experimental melting and refining. A full report will be forthcoming in a publication of the Institute for Archaeo-Metallurgical Studies.

REFERENCES

Craddock, P.T. 1980. The Composition of Copper Produced at the Ancient Smelting Camps in the Wadi Timna, Israel, in *Scientific Studies in Early Mining and Extractive Metallurgy,* ed. by Craddock, P.T. British Museum Occasional Paper No. 20, pp. 165-175.

Tylecote, R.F., Ghaznavi, H.A., and Boydell, P.J. 1977. Partitioning of Trace Elements Between the Ores, Fluxes, Slags and Metal During the Smelting of Copper. *Journal of Archaeological Science,* 4: 305-333.

Tylecote, R.F. and Boydell, P.J. 1978. Experiments on Copper Smelting, in *Chalcolithic Copper Smelting,* with B. Rothenberg. IAMS Monograph No. 1, London, pp. 27-49.

THE MEANING OF *BARZEL* IN THE BIBLICAL EXPRESSIONS "CHARIOTS OF IRON", "YOKE OF IRON", ETC.

John F.A. Sawyer
Department of Religious Studies
University of Newcastle upon Tyne

In a study of the iron implements used by King David in his treatment of the Ammonites (2 Sam. 12:31) I proposed that *barzel* "iron" in that context and in others (e.g. Deut. 4:20; 28:48; Amos 1:3) has peculiarly ugly or frightening associations /1/. Further investigations in the light of recent archaeo-metallurgy now provide striking confirmation of that suggestion /2/.

Analysis of iron artifacts from ancient Palestine, Assyria and Persia has conclusively shown that the manufacture of iron tools and weapons was still at a fairly primitive stage in most if not all parts of the ancient near east until as late as the ninth or even eighth century BC /3/. Eighth century iron blades from Nimrud, for example, where one might have expected a reasonably high standard of craftsmanship under the Assyrian authorities, are of poor quality: the hard, carburized part of the blade is near the centre while the cutting edge is weak and inefficient /4/. It was clearly a hit-or-miss affair, showing that the smiths were not yet in command of the complex processes and techniques necessary for the production of tempered steel. The change from bronze to iron was thus not due to the superior efficiency of iron, as is often assumed, but to other factors including the unavailability of tin /5/. There is no archaeological evidence that the Philistines' superiority over the Israelites (cf. I Sam. 13:19ff.) was due to their monopoly of iron /6/. Single pieces of high quality iron do occur on Early Iron Age sites, but these are exceptions, due for the most part to chance, and were no doubt greatly treasured by their owners. On the archaeological evidence available at present it seems virtually impossible that efficient iron tools or weapons could have been produced on anything like a large scale much before the ninth century BC. I want to argue that the Biblical evidence agrees substantially with this picture.

Early references to efficient iron metallurgy are likely
to be rare and to express awe and wonderment at its peculiar
qualities of toughness, sharpness and heaviness in contrast to
bronze.   The description of the Philistine hero Goliath in
1 Sam. 17 is a perfect example: his helmet, coat of mail,
greaves and javelin were of bronze, while his spearhead, which
weighed 600 shekels, the climax of this description, was of
iron.   The proportion of iron to bronze in this description
exactly corresponds to the archaeological picture at many Iron
I sites in Palestine and elsewhere, and may actually be one
detail in the ancient legend which corresponds to historical
reality.   Another example from early legend is the miracle of
the floating axe-head in 2 Kgs. 6:1-7.   The miraculous element
in the story should not be allowed to obscure the details of
everyday life recorded incidentally in it: the axehead is
termed simply *ha-barzel* "the iron" (cf. Deut. 19:5) and its
special value is emphasised by the woodman's consternation when
it accidentally comes off and falls in the water: "Alas!", he
cried, "it was borrowed."   The loss of a high quality iron
axehead, that would last many years, frequently sharpened, was
a serious matter.   No doubt its heaviness would also add to the
effect of the miracle story, but its rarity and peculiar value
in a small rural community are the most striking features
against the metallurgical background we have been discussing.
The "iron bedstead" of King Og of Bashan (Deut. 3:11) may be
another example from early legend of a rare, memorable piece
of iron metallurgy, but there is another explanation possible
(see below).

Apart from these two or three rare instances, iron does not
figure prominently in early descriptions of normal everyday
life.   It is not until later texts that *barzel* appears as an
everyday metal.   A conspicuous illustration of this is to be
found by comparing the law banning the use of a metal implement
in the building of an altar in Exod. 20:25, where the metal is
unspecified, with the parallel in Deut. 27:5, where iron is
specially mentioned as though by then it was in common use.
Josh. 8:31 and the still later Num. 35:16 are other examples.
Among the metals employed in the building of the Temple, iron
is conspicuous by its absence from the earlier account (I Kgs.
6-7), but is mentioned 8 times in the later Chronicles account
(I Chron. 22-23; 29:2,2,7; 2 Chron. 2:6,13; 24:12).   Iron takes
its place among imports and exports only in late texts (e.g.
Isa. 60:17; Jer. 6:28; Ezek. 27:19).   The toughness of iron
that "breaks to pieces and shatters all things" is assumed in

the dream of Nebuchadnezzar from a still later date (Dan. 2:40).
All this exactly corresponds to the archaeological evidence.

A large proportion of the occurrences of *barzel*, however,
do not fit the archaeological evidence. It is historically
highly improbable, for example, that the Canaanites were
equipped with iron chariots before the end of the second
millennium BC (Josh. 17:16,18; Judg. 1:19; 4:3,13), or that in
David's day iron was the normal metal for the production of
other equipment (II Sam. 12:31). If the mention of iron in
these and many other passages is not historical, then why is
the term used and does the archaeological picture help us to
understand its meaning?

A recurring feature in many passages in which *barzel* occurs,
but not $n^e hoshet$ "bronze" or any other metal, is iron's
unmistakeable association with, at best, ugliness, obstinacy
and hostility, at worst, oppression, fighting, smashing and
torture. Such passages occur in all parts of the Old Testament
and with reference to all periods, from the "iron-furnace" of
Egypt (e.g. Deut. 4:20; I Kgs. 8:51; Jer. 11:4) and the
Canaanites' awesome chariots just referred to, to the
devastating iron in Nebuchadnezzar's dream (Dan. 2:40). Iron
makes an effective rod for beating the enemies of Israel
(Ps. 2:9), the chains of slavery (Ps. 107:10; cf. 105:18) and
the instruments of brutal torture mentioned earlier (II Sam.
12:31). All the evidence suggests that the word *barzel*, in
most of the Biblical passages where it occurs, was an emotive
term, with unmistakeably hostile and aggressive associations.
The reasons for this are not hard to find.

In the first place, *barzel*, unlike $n^e hoshet$ "bronze,
copper", is a word of foreign origin, with no Hebrew or Semitic
etymology identifiable /7/. In many cases the etymological
data are irrelevant, but here the foreign origin of the word
barzel seems to give added effect to its recurring usage in
connection with Israel's barbaric enemies. Egyptians (Deut.
4:20), Amorites (Deut. 3:11), Canaanites (Josh. 17:16,18),
Philistines (I Sam. 17:7), Syrians (Amos 1:3), Assyrians (Isa.
10:34), Babylonians (Jer. 15:12) and Greeks (Dan. 2:40) all
have at least one mention in this category. David's ally
Barzillai (the only derivative of *barzel*, incidentally, in
Biblical Hebrew) was a Gileadite (2 Sam. 17:27ff.; cf. 19:31ff.),
and it may be significant that his descendants were excluded by
name from the priesthood as unclean (Ezra 2:61f.; Neh. 7:63f.),

in spite of their ancestor's good relations with David. Gilead
was actually an important source of iron (Josephus, *War* 4.454;
Mishna, *Succ.* 3.1), and this may be the origin of the name
Barzillai. The foreign origin of iron is still remarked upon
in a relatively late passage (Jer. 15:12). The fact that most
of the enemy yokes, chariots, chains, instruments of torture
and other implements are iron, not bronze or some other metal,
according to Biblical tradition, cannot be a historical matter,
as we have seen, in the majority of cases. It is a lexical
matter: n^e*hoshet,* a pure Semitic term with several derivatives,
is more frequent in all periods than *barzel,* and, as far as
one can judge, entirely without its hostile, barbaric
associations. Both the actual origin of the iron technology
and the origin of the word are foreign, and this seems to have
been one factor in the choice of *barzel,* over and over again,
in the context of foreign aggression and oppression, in
preference to the historically more accurate term n^e*hoshet*
"bronze".

A second factor was probably the poor quality of most of
the iron artifacts throughout much of the period covered by the
Old Testament texts. Not only were they as a rule clumsier and
uglier than bronze; they were also, in the early period
particularly, of inferior quality. Techniques of carburization
and quenching were not sufficiently developed to make iron
weapons and equipment a dangerous new threat: iron played little
part in Israel's wars /8/.

It may be that unsuccessful iron technology and frequent
failure on the part of iron smiths to produce what society
demanded led to a third factor in the development of iron's
pejorative overtones: the ingratitude, hostility and scorn with
which the smith was popularly regarded. This phenomenon is
well known from many societies, not only primitive ones, and
it applies, as has often been noted, particularly to the iron
smith /9/. His dirty, frightening and often, one might add,
unsuccessful work, and the soot, smoke, sparks, heat, bellows
and hammering in his smithy frequently attracted suspicion and
hatred. It seems likely that the comparison of Israel's house
of bondage in Egypt to an "iron furnace" (Deut. 4:20; I Kgs.
8:51; Jer. 11:4) owed something to this popular impression of
the working conditions of the blacksmith. An Old Testament
example can be added to many other descriptions to confirm this:

"So too the smith sitting by the anvil,
   intent upon his handiwork in iron;
the breath of the fire melts his flesh,
   and he wastes away in the heat of the
      furnace
and he inclines his ear to the sound of
      the hammer ..."
               (Sir. 38:28; cf. Isa. 44:12)

The ambivalent attitude to the smith, who incidentally was
frequently a foreigner, is reflected too in Genesis 4 in
connection with Cain and Lamech, father of the first smith,
Tubal-Cain /10/. Together with its foreign origin, then, the
inferior quality of much iron metallurgy, and its ugly
appearance, this attitude of fear and hostility towards the
smith probably contributed to the ugly overtones of the word
barzel. It was an emotive term, suggesting, in almost all its
occurrences, foreign aggression and brutality.

Of course, Israel could turn this hostile metal against her
enemies, as David did when he used "iron picks and axes" against
the Ammonites (II Sam. 12:31), or Zedekiah ben Imlah when he
made for himself "horns of iron", and said, "Thus says the Lord,
With these you shall push the Syrians until they are destroyed"
(I Kgs. 22:11). The Lord cuts down the mighty like trees with
an iron axe (Isa. 10:34), and breaks the king's enemies with a
"rod of iron" (Ps. 2:9).

Finally, it has often been pointed out that the nine-foot
long "bedstead" of King Og of Bashan (Deut. 3:11) is unlikely to
have been made of iron. The reading *bazelet* "basalt" has been
proposed and the idea of a basalt sarcophagus introduced. If
such was the original reading, however, it is none the less
interesting to ask what the text as it stands means. It may be
a scribal error, but, in view of the evidence for the deliberate
choice of the term *barzel* in such contexts, it is more probable
that this is another example of the polemical usage we have
been examining. Where any other monarch would lie, either
before or after his death, upon a bed of gold or bronze or
carved wood, King Og of Bashan lay on some ugly iron object, as
befitted his barbaric foreign origins.

NOTES

/1/ "David's treatment of the Ammonites (II Samuel 12:31).
A Study in the history of interpretation", *Trans. Glasg. Univ.
Orient. Society* 26 (1978), pp. 96-107, esp. pp. 102f.
/2/ I gratefully acknowledge criticisms and advice from
Dr Albert Wraith, Department of Metallurgy, University of
Newcastle upon Tyne.
/3/ See especially Jane C. Waldbaum, *From Bronze to Iron:
The Transition from the Bronze Age to the Iron Age in the
Eastern Mediterranean, Stud. Med. Arch.* 54 (Goteborg, 1978),
chaps. 3 and 4; also "The first archaeological appearance of
iron and the transition to the Iron Age", in *The Coming of the
Age of Iron,* eds. T.A. Wertime and J.D. Muhly (Yale Univ. Press,
New Haven and London, 1980), pp. 82ff.
/4/ R. Pleiner, "The technology of three Assyrian Iron
Artifacts from Khorsabad", *Journ. Near East. Stud.* 38 (1979),
pp. 83-91.
/5/ Waldbaum, *From Bronze to Iron,* pp. 67-73; R.F. Tylecote,
A History of Metallurgy, Metals Society, London, 1976, pp. 40f.
/6/ Waldbaum, *op. cit.,* pp. 42ff.; *Coming of the Age of Iron,*
pp. 84f.
/7/ *Hebräisches und Aramäisches Lexikon zum Alten Testament*[3],
ed. W. Baumgartner (Leiden, 1976), pp. 148f. (with full
bibliography).
/8/ Evidence for intentional carburizing by 1000 BC, however,
is increasing: see T.S. Wheeler and R. Maddin, "Metallurgy and
ancient man", in *The Coming of the Age of Iron,* pp. 99-126,
esp. pp. 121ff.
/9/ Cf. R.J. Forbes, *Studies in Ancient Technology,* Vol. VIII
(Rev. ed., Leiden, 1971), Chap. 3; M. Eliade, *The Forge and the
Crucible* (London, 1962), esp. pp. 25f.
/10/ J.F.A. Sawyer, "Relics of metal-working traditions in
Genesis 4", paper read at 56th Summer Meeting of Society for
Old Testament Study, Sheffield, 1980.
/11/ G.R. Driver, in *New English Bible,* ad loc. (cf.
Baumgartner's *Hebräisches und Aramäisches Lexikon,* p. 149).
/12/ The possibility that Neo-Assyrian *parzillu* "iron" had
similar overtones in some contexts is discussed by R. Pleiner
and J.K. Bjorkman, "The Assyrian Iron Age", *Proc. Amer. Phil.
Soc.* 118 (1974), pp. 283-313, esp. p. 305. K.H. Singer in a
recent monograph, *Die Metalle Gold, Silber, Kupfer und Eisen im
Alten Testament and ihre Symbolik, Forschung zur Bibel* 43
(Echter Verlag, 1980), stresses the efficiency of iron (p. 185)
as the source of its frightening associations, and says little
about its foreignness and the social attitudes involved.

THE 'UNITED' CAMPAIGN AGAINST MOAB IN 2 KINGS 3:4-27

John R. Bartlett
School of Hebrew, Biblical and Theological Studies
Trinity College
Dublin
Republic of Ireland

One of the major problems for any historian of the land east of the Jordan in the Biblical period is that nearly all the literary evidence comes from elsewhere and reflects the interests of other peoples. The Moabite stone is a glorious exception: if only we had something similar from Edom! Perhaps one day something will turn up; meanwhile, we must do the best we can with the historical records of Edom's enemies - Judah, Assyria, and Babylon. My present purpose is to examine the narrative of 2 Kings 3:4-27, which tells of a campaign led by Jehoram of Israel against Moab in the mid-ninth century B.C. In this campaign a part is said to have been played by an unnamed king of Edom.

There is more to the narrative of 2 Kings 3 than at first meets the eye. It is clearly not designed or presented as a simple military or political record. It is presented as one of a long sequence of stories about the major prophets Elijah and Elisha. The focus of the story in 2 Kings 3 is on the part played by the prophet Elisha and the word of the Lord which comes from him. And it is particularly interesting that this story both in outline and in detail is remarkably similar to the famous story of Micaiah ben Imlah in 1 Kings 22. In both stories the king of Israel (Ahab in 1 Kings 22, Jehoram in 2 Kings 3) invites Jehoshaphat king of Judah to accompany him on a campaign (against Syria at Ramoth-gilead in 1 Kings 22, against Moab in 2 Kings 3). In each case Jehoshaphat replies that he will go with the same words: 'I am as you are, my people as your people, my horses as your horses'. In each case Jehoshaphat asks for a prophet through whom they might enquire of the Lord (1 Kings 22:5,7; 2 Kings 3:11). In the first case, Micaiah, after being warned to speak as favourably as the prophets of the king, invites the king to 'go up and triumph; the Lord will give it into the hand of the king', but goes on to make it clear, in a further oracle and in his marvellous exit line, that 'If you return in peace, the Lord has not spoken by me'. In the second narrative, Elisha like Micaiah makes it clear that he has no time for the court prophets favoured by the king of Israel and his predecessors (v. 13) or for the king himself (v. 14). He then predicts, first, that water will be supplied to meet the armies' present need in the wilderness (vv. 8f., 16f.), and secondly, that the Lord 'will also give the Moabites into your hand, and you shall conquer every fortified city, and every choice city, and shall fell every good tree, and stop up all the springs of water, and ruin every good piece of land with stones' (vv. 18f.). These two predictions are fulfilled in vv. 20, 25. Elisha appears to predict success, and success follows - until we reach the unexpected end of the story in vv. 26f.:

> When the king of Moab saw that the battle was going against him, he took with him seven hundred swordsmen to break through, opposite the king of Edom; but they could not. Then he took his eldest son who was to reign in his stead, and offered him for a burnt offering upon the wall. And there came great wrath upon Israel; and they withdrew from him and returned to their own land.

Similarly in 1 Kings 22:36, at the end of a day of battle against the Syrians,

> About sunset, a cry went through the army, 'Every man to his city, and every man to his country!'

Recently S.J. de Vries has more closely examined the relationship between 1 Kings 22 and 2 Kings 3, and argues that 2 Kings 3: 5b-25a displays close affinities both in content and form with one of two narrative strands to be found in 1 Kings 22 ('Narrative A', vv. 2b-4a, 4b-9, 15-18, 26-37), and is dependent upon it. He notes also the presence of schematic elements in 2 Kings 3 - the three kings, the seven days' march, the conquering of every city, felling of every tree, stopping up of all the waters - and of typical characters - Elisha the model prophet, Jehoshaphat the godly king, the king of Israel as the exponent of unbelief. He finds that the narrative is arranged chiastically, beginning and ending with military action against

Moab, and including the carefully worked out motif of the
Israelite thirst for water, the provision of which becomes the
means by which the Moabites are led to disaster. He argues
finally that the prophetic legend of verses 5b-25a has been
further developed by the addition of a later historical
framework in verses 4-5a and 25b-27.

What this means for our investigation is that the account
of 2 Kings 3:5b-25a cannot be treated simply as a straightforward
description of a campaign and a political situation. Its
relationship with 1 Kings 22 is not accidental. The historian
is using accounts of Israel's military campaigns against Syria
and Moab (both of them failures for Israel) to illustrate and
underline his major point that the word of the Lord as spoken
to Israel by the prophets does not always support the political
aims of the kings of Israel. As is well known, the
Deuteronomistic historian did not favour the kings of Israel,
who are condemned for following the sin of Jeroboam the son of
Nebat. On the other hand, the historian represents Jehoshaphat
as the good king who 'walked in the ways of Asa his father; he
did not turn aside from it, doing what was right in the sight
of the Lord' (1 Kings 22:43), just as Asa in turn 'did what was
right in the sight of the Lord, as David his father had done'
(1 Kings 15:11). It is interesting that Jehoshaphat is said to
have 'made peace with Israel' (1 Kings 22:44) and indeed to
have identified himself and his people with Israel ('I am as
you are, my people as your people') and fought with Israel. It
is noticeable that in these joint campaigns against Syria and
Moab, in each case it is only Israel that suffers; Jehoshaphat
disappears from view in the final episodes. Possibly the
historian is indicating that Jehoshaphat and Judah did
themselves no good by associating with the kings of Israel - a
point underlined later by the Chronicler in his adaptation of
the story of Jehoshaphat's refusal to cooperate with Ahaziah of
Israel in naval affairs (1 Kings 22:48f.; cf. 2 Chron. 20:35-37).
If so, it is also possible that the historian is similarly
indicating that Jehoshaphat as king of Judah will do himself no
good by associating with the arch-enemy Edom; Edom in Israelite
tradition had a bad reputation for violence and treachery.

It is with the place of Edom in the events described in
2 Kings 3 that this paper is particularly concerned. It must
be said that on political grounds Edom's participation in a
campaign against Moab is not impossible. Whether Edom was
Judah's vassal at the time, or an independent kingdom, she would

doubtless view the development of a strong and independent Moab
on her northern frontier with some concern. Where Moab was
concerned, Edom's interests coincided with Israel's. Israel
herself was not unaware of the advantages of connections with
the south, as is shown by the narrative of 1 Kings 22:48f., in
which Ahaziah of Israel proposes to Jehoshaphat that they
cooperate in the shipping venture from Ezion-geber. It is
possible that Jehoram sought Edomite help in his campaign
against Moab; he may at least, perhaps, have wished for
permission to march across Edomite territory, for the march
was 'by way of the wilderness of Edom'. This is, however, an
unusual designation, and needs some consideration. The phrase
is often taken to refer to the region east of Edom (cf. Gray,
1970, 485; Aharoni, 1979, 58), though Aharoni thinks it is a
mistake for 'the road to Edom' which descended from Arad via
Kh. Ghazzeh past the north end of Jebel Usdum to the Arabah.
But the geography of the campaign is more than a little vague.
It may be that the 'circuitous march of seven days' suggests,
as Gray thinks, that the army is making a great detour to the
east of Edom. But I suspect that the author has in mind,
whether consciously or subconsciously, the account of Numbers
20, in which the story of the attempt of the children of Israel
to pass through Edom, with its fields, vineyards, wells, and
highway, is preceded by a wandering in the wilderness (Num. 20:
2-13) where there is no water to drink and the people complain
that they and their cattle are about to die; Moses strikes the
rock, water comes abundantly, and the congregation drink, and
their cattle. The account of 2 Kings 3 reflects the same theme:
the Israelites enter the region of the wilderness near Edom,
on a circuitous march, run short of water - they even have
cattle (v. 17) with them, though surely an invading army would
expect to get its meat by raiding - and a prophetic figure
provides water in abundance. The geography of this story is
not real until we reach Kir-hareseth in verse 25. The location
of the route-march in the wilderness of Edom has at least as
much to do with the prophetic and theological element in this
account as it has with the historical and geographical; and
while I grant that in theory Edom might have been grateful for
Israelite success in limiting the power of Mesha of Moab, in
fact I doubt whether the king of Edom and the Edomites played
much part in the original campaign.

The reference in 2 Kings 3 to the king of Edom is itself
highly suspect. We know that when David occupied Edom, c.990
BC (Bartlett, 1976, 219f.), the Edomites became 'David's

servants' and the land was garrisoned (2 Sam. 8:14). There is
no mention of any king surviving as David's vassal, and it is
most unlikely that any did. We hear of the escape of a certain
Hadad, 'of the royal house in Edom', to Egypt, where he is said
to have married the sister of the Pharaoh and produced a son
Genubath. He apparently returned to Edom (against the wishes
of Pharaoh) to become 'an adversary against Solomon'. But
there is no indication that he was particularly successful, or
that he left behind a dynastic successor. He must in any case
have been dead by about 925 BC if he was a boy c.990 BC, and
the next we hear of any government in Edom is the brief note
in 1 Kings 22:47, 'There was no king in Edom'. This refers to
the period of Jehoshaphat's reign, perhaps, to judge from the
reference to Ahaziah son of Ahab in verse 49, towards the end
of the reign. So far the text is clear, but the following words
in the Hebrew provide a number of puzzles. The Hebrew reads
$niṣṣab$ $melek:$ $y^{e}hôšapaṭ$ $ʿāśār$ $ʾoniyyôt$ $taršîš$ $lāleket$ ...
What does $niṣṣab$ $melek$ mean, and how does it relate to what
precedes and what follows? One might take $niṣṣab$ alone with
the preceding words, as does the LXX, and translate, 'There was
no king appointed in Edom. King Jehoshaphat made ships ...'
One might take the phrase as it stands, with the RSV (cf. NEB),
and translate, 'There was no king in Edom; a deputy was king.
And Jehoshaphat made ...' Or one might repoint and read
$n^{e}ṣib$ $melek,$ translating, 'a deputy of king Jehoshaphat made
ships ...' However we construe the words, it is clear that at
that time there was no Edomite king in Edom. Possibly an
appointee of Jehoshaphat governed in Edom; or possibly the text
says only that an appointee of Jehoshaphat made (if $ʿāśār$ can be
emended to $ʿāśāh$) ships (or, a ship) with the intention of
trading in Ophir. That there was no native king in Edom in
Jehoshaphat's day is confirmed by the notice in 2 Kings 8:20
that in the days of Jehoshaphat's son Jehoram of Judah 'Edom
revolted from the rule of Judah and set up a king of their own'.
In short, we know of no king of Edom between David's conquest
of Edom and Edom's regaining of independence in the reign of
Jehoram of Judah. This poses a problem for the account of
2 Kings 3, which refers to the existence of a king of Edom in
the days of Jehoshaphat.

There are several ways in which this problem can be
resolved. If one accepts the statement of 2 Kings 3:9 that
'the king of Israel (Jehoram) went with the king of Judah
(Jehoshaphat) and the king of Edom', then one solution might
be to suppose, with Thiele, Gray and others, that there was a

co-regency of Jehoshaphat and Jehoram of Judah. Thiele (1951, 205) dates this from 853-848 BC. In this case, Edom's rebellion could be put at the beginning of Jehoram's co-regency, and the campaign of 2 Kings 3 could be put a year or two later, Judah's army being led on this campaign by the senior partner of the co-regency, Jehoshaphat - or perhaps the historian, knowing that the campaign took place within Jehoshaphat's lifetime, simply assumed that Jehoshaphat led the army of Judah. But this whole solution seems to me rather forced. It depends above all on the thesis of a co-regency. Not every chronological scheme suggested for the divided monarchy demands a co-regency here, and Miller (1967, 278f.) argues that the alleged evidence for a co-regency (2 Kings 3:1; cf. 2 Kings 1:17) only arose because in the redaction of the story of the invasion of Moab the king of Judah was wrongly identified as Jehoshaphat. Once this had happened, Jehoshaphat's reign was made to overlap that of Jehoram of Israel. The correct chronology, Miller argues, was preserved by the Lucianic recension of the Septuagint, and by the synchronism of 2 Kings 1:17 (MT), according to which Jehoram of Israel became king in the second year of Jehoram of Judah.

This leads naturally to the second solution proposed, that the narrative of 2 Kings 3 did not originally identify the king of Judah as Jehoshaphat, but as Ahaziah, who followed Jehoram of Judah and was killed by Jehu. If the Edomites made a king for themselves in Jehoram's reign, there could certainly have been a king of Edom ready to campaign with Israel against Moab in Ahaziah's reign. This solution depends on the Lucianic recension, which (i) ignores the synchronism of 2 Kings 3:1 which puts the start of the reign of Jehoram of Israel in Jehoshaphat's 18th year, and (ii) refers to Ahaziah, not Jehoshaphat, as the king of Judah in 2 Kings 3 (for details, see J.D. Shenkel, 1968, 93-101; de Vries, 1980, 88). This case, argued independently by Miller (1967) and Shenkel (1968), is attractive, but the thesis that the Lucianic recension of the LXX has preserved the older tradition of the chronology of the books of Kings is inherently less likely than the more obvious thesis that the Lucianic recension has observed the difficulties of the MT chronology and attempted to correct it - in this case by omitting the awkward synchronism in 2 Kings 3:1 and replacing Jehoshaphat with the obviously possible Ahaziah. (For criticism of Shenkel's case, see Gooding, 1970, 118-131; de Vries, 1980, 88, 108). De Vries (1980, 88) has recently argued strongly that 'the name "Jehoshaphat" has to be original

in the three contexts (verses 11, 12a, 12b) where it appears
without the title "king of Judah", unless we suppose that it
has been substituted for another proper name - an arbitary
assumption'.

The question of the names of the kings in this story is
a difficult one, because it really depends upon one's view of
how 2 Kings 3 was put together - by whom, and from what sources?
These are questions to which we must return, but if we may
suppose for the moment that, basically, a prophetic tale has
been built on to an archival note about Mesha of Moab and his
rebellion after Ahab's death, reference to Jehoram of Israel is
hardly surprising (Ahaziah, Ahab's immediate successor lasted
only about a year) and is supported by Elisha's reference in
2 Kings 3:13 to 'the prophets of your father and the prophets of
your mother', apparently referring to Ahab and Jezebel. The
name Jehoram itself may have been added secondarily to the text
(cf. Noth, 1957, 83: Shenkel, 1968, 99; de Vries, 1980, 108),
but very understandably. The reference to Jehoshaphat in this
story (and the accompanying synchronism of 2 Kings 3:1) is less
immediately intelligible, particularly as the historian has
already reported Jehoshaphat's death (1 Kings 22:50) and
Jehoram's accession, but in view of the similarity we have
noticed between the account of 2 Kings 3 and that of 1 Kings 22,
it seems most likely that the presence of Jehoshaphat in 2 Kings
3 is related to his presence in 1 Kings 22:1-38. It has been
shown by a number of scholars that the Syrian campaigns
described in 1 Kings 20 and 1 Kings 22:1-38 really belong to a
later reign than that of Ahab, for Ahab was on friendly terms
with Syria, and it was not until later that the Syrians under
Hazael invaded Gilead (2 Kings 10:32). King Ahab of Israel
died peacefully (such is the implication of the phrase 'So
Ahab slept with his fathers' in 1 Kings 22:40; see Miller, 1966,
445; de Vries, 1980, 97-99), but the king of Israel who
campaigned in 1 Kings 22 died in his chariot of an arrow wound
received in battle at Ramoth-gilead (1 Kings 22:34f.).
2 Kings 8:28f., however, makes it clear that it was Ahab's
son Jehoram who was wounded at Ramoth-gilead, and 2 Kings 9:24
tells how Jehu 'shot Joram between the shoulders, so that the
arrow pierced his heart, and he sank in his chariot'. It is
hard to resist de Vries' conclusion that '1 Kings 22 has been
developed from the historical background of the events recorded
in 2 Kings 8:28ff.' (1980, 99) though indeed Miller (1966,
441-454) makes a case that the battles in 1 Kings 20, 22, and
2 Kings 3 refer in fact to the reign of Jehoahaz the son of Jehu.

In either case, the point for our purpose is that in 1 Kings 22 the historian has attributed to Jehoshaphat's reign a campaign which did not belong there, and that something similar has happened in the closely related 2 Kings 3, where Jehoshaphat is portrayed in a very similar manner and given a very similar role in the story. The attribution of these events to Jehoshaphat's reign may have been made all the easier for the historian by his knowledge or belief that 'Jehoshaphat made peace with the king of Israel' (1 Kings 22:40). Another element in the attribution of these events to Jehoshaphat's reign is the writer's clearly visible aim of contrasting the religious attitudes of the king of Israel and the king of Judah. The king of Israel has no faith (v. 10) and is contemptuously referred by Elisha to the prophets of his parents Ahab and Jezebel, while the king of Judah shows great confidence (v. 7) and asks for a prophet of the Lord. Jehoram of Judah was clearly not regarded by the Deuteronomistic historian as fitting this role (see 2 Kings 8:17f.), but his father Jehoshaphat, as we have seen, was eminently suitable (1 Kings 22:43).

It should be noted in passing that the fact that the Deuteronomistic historian (or a subsequent editor) has set this story in Jehoshaphat's reign, identifying the king of Judah with Jehoshaphat, does not necessarily mean that the name Jehoshaphat has entered the text secondarily. On the contrary it was almost certainly in the text of 2 Kings 3 from the start - from the moment that the historian incorporated the tale at this point. As M. Weippert has pointed out, the kings are naturally given their names at the beginning of the story; after that the titles 'king of Moab', 'king of Israel' are adequate for the most part, except sometimes in the introduction of speech. In verse 12b, where Jehoshaphat's name intrudes oddly in the row of titles, the original may have read 'the king of Judah' (Noth, 1957, 83; Weippert, 1971, 316). The prophetic tale used by the historian probably referred only to 'the king of Israel' and 'the king of Judah' without naming them; C.F. Burney long ago derived the accounts of 1 Kings 20, 1 Kings 22, and 2 Kings 3:4-27, 6:8-23, 24-33, and 2 Kings 7 from the same source partly on the ground that all these passages used the title *melek yiśrā'ēl* (Burney, 1903, 207-215).

It seems likely, then, that the historical difficulty caused by the reference to 'the king of Edom' in the context of Jehoshaphat's reign can be solved by the demonstration that the events described in 2 Kings 3 have been somewhat artificially

linked with Jehoshaphat. This is far, however, from being the
whole answer. We still need to examine the part played by the
king of Edom in this account, and to consider further what
actual historical event might lie behind this account.

It must be said that the king of Edom plays a very small
part in the story. He is not identified (though the other
protagonists are). There is no reference to him in the
planning of the campaign by the king of Israel and the king of
Judah. Jehoram of Israel proposes to march 'by the way of the
wilderness of Edom' (v. 8), and in the next verse we read: 'so
the king of Israel went with the king of Judah and the king of
Edom'. In verse 12 we read that the king of Edom accompanies
the other two kings to meet Elisha. In verse 20 we are told
that the promised water came from 'the direction of Edom', and
in verse 22 'the Moabites saw the water opposite them as red as
blood ('adummîm kaddām). And they said, "This is blood".' Here
we have a clear punning reference to Edom (for a similar pun,
cf. Gen. 25:25). It seems quite evident that it is the *land* of
Edom that is important in this story, not the king of Edom and
his military power, and the reference to the king of Edom in
verses 9 and 12 is probably inspired solely by the immediately
previous reference to the geographical area in which the
campaign takes place. (And as we have seen, the geography of
the account may have been drawn from the narrative of Numbers
ch. 20.) The narrator of 2 Kings 3 knows of no specific
activity that he can ascribe to the king of Edom in this
campaign, and it is likely that he was brought into the story,
whether at the time of its connection with Jehoshaphat, or, as
is more likely, at some earlier point, simply because the
story-teller thought he ought to be there if the campaign was
taking place across Edomite territory. At all events, the
reference to the king of Edom suggests that the story took
shape sometime after Edom became independent in the reign of
Jehoram of Judah and acquired her own king.

One other reference to Edom in this story requires
consideration. In 2 Kings 3:26, 'when the king of Moab saw
that the battle was going against him, he took with him seven
hundred swordsmen to break through, opposite the king of Edom;
but they could not.' The Hebrew phrase 'el melek 'edôm has
been variously interpreted. In the context of a story in which
the king of Edom is allied with Israel and therefore Moab's
enemy, the phrase has been taken to mean 'against the king of
Edom', with hostile intent, or 'towards the king of Edom', as a

possible if unwilling ally, or, as in the RSV, 'opposite the
king of Edom', in a merely neutral sense describing the place
where the king tried to break through. A number of scholars
have followed the Old Latin and read 'Aram' for 'Edom', with the
comment that Damascus would have been the Moabite king's natural
ally (see Montgomery and Gehman, 1951, 313). In this case the
reference to the king of Edom disappears; in the former case,
the king of Edom is given a role (though a passive one) at the
end of the story, but his presence may still be explained along
the lines argued above.

In my view, then, the account of 2 Kings 3 provides no
solid evidence for the presence of the king of Edom in any
campaign involving king Jehoshaphat of Judah and king Jehoram
of Israel against king Mesha of Moab. The fact that the unnamed
king of Edom could feature in the account reveals that the
account belongs to a period after the reign of Jehoram of Judah
when the existence of Edomite kings could be taken for granted.
The king of Edom was probably brought into the story simply
because the story was associated with the wilderness of Edom
where the water appeared, appropriately, red as blood. And the
presence in the story of the wilderness of Edom may owe something
to the comparable account of the waterless wanderings of the
Israelites in the wilderness near Edom in Numbers 20. If we
can thus dispose of the presence of the king of Edom in the
original story of this campaign, we free ourselves of some
awkward historical problems. And we are now free to place
Jehoram's campaign against Moab in its proper historical context.

Prophetic legend apart, the historical core of 2 Kings 3 is
surely to be found in the notice of the king of Moab's rebellion
after the death of Ahab, and Jehoram of Israel's response. There
seems no reason to doubt this. If Mesha rebelled soon after the
death of Ahab, or even before it, it would take some time, as
M. Weippert has pointed out (1971, 318), for his non-payment of
tribute to register in Samaria, and a little more to organise
the Israelite response. Ahab's immediate successor Ahaziah
probably did not have time to react to Mesha, for his reign was
short, perhaps only a few months either side of a new year
(1 Kings 22:51). When he came to the throne, Jehoshaphat of
Judah was still on his throne (1 Kings 22:48f.); but by the end
of Ahaziah's short reign, Jehoshaphat had been succeeded by
Jehoram (2 Kings 1:17). Israel's response to Moab's rebellion
was thus made (perhaps as late as 849 BC; cf. Liver, 1967, 14-31)
by Jehoram of Israel, and Jehoshaphat of Judah could have been

involved only if we revert to the thesis of his co-regency with
his son Jehoram of Judah. It seems to me better to accept only
the limited account of 2 Kings 3:4-6, in which Jehoram musters
Israel against Moab, and to suppose, for reasons we have already
considered, that the prophetic tale involving Jehoshaphat (and
the king of Edom) is a later graft onto an early archival
account.

The prophetic tale, focussing on the fulfilment of Elisha's
prophecy, really begins with verse 7 and ends with verse 25,
which fulfils Elisha's prophecy of verses 18f. in every
particular, 'until Kir-hareseth (alone) was left, and the
slingers surrounded it and smote it' (for the text, and the
omission of the reference to the stones, see Montgomery and
Gehman, 1951, 363). Clearly the Israelites are successful, as
Elisha had said they would be, for the sake of king Jehoshaphat
and in spite of the unbelief of the king of Israel. But the
author of the present account of 2 Kings 3, modelling himself
on the account in 1 Kings 22, has built onto this prophetic tale
an ending which surprisingly reverses the Israelite victory, and
the Israelites, as in 1 Kings 22, are forced to withdraw. This
ending is inconsistent with the tale, but presupposes it, and
must have come from the hand of the historian who incorporated
the accounts of 1 Kings 20, 22, and 2 Kings 3 into the major
history of 1 and 2 Kings, whether he was the deuteronomistic
historian himself or a subsequent editor. While this ending
serves to underline the historian's view that the house of Omri
had incurred the divine wrath by their activities, it is not
necessarily legendary in content; and if it were legendary, it
nevertheless might preserve the memory that Israel's campaign
against Moab under Jehoram had not been successful. Basically,
the historian knew of the Moabite king's rebellion, and of
Jehoram's unsuccessful response. He has filled out his account
with a prophetic tale about Elisha which told how in accordance
with Elisha's prophecy the king of Israel - Jehoram, later in
his reign? - campaigned successfully against Moab, and he has
adjusted this to the known facts by the dramatic story of the
Moabite king's sacrifice of his son on the wall, and its
results. We may be left asking whether the story of Elisha's
prophecy and its results reflects an actual success of the king
of Israel against Moab at some stage in the history of Moab's
struggle for independence, and if so, at what date, but that is
another day's work.

BIBLIOGRAPHY

J.R. Bartlett 1976	'An adversary against Solomon, Hadad the Edomite', *ZAW* 88, 205-226.
C.F. Burney 1903	*Notes on the Hebrew text of the Books of Kings* (Oxford).
D.W. Gooding 1970	review of J.D. Shenkel, *Chronology and recensional development in the Greek text of Kings, JTS* ns 21, 118-131.
J. Liver 1967	'The wars of Mesha, king of Moab', *PEQ* 99, 14-31.
B.O. Long 1973	'2 Kings iii. and the genre of prophetic narrative', *VT* 23, 337-348.
J.M. Miller 1966	'The Elisha cycle and the accounts of the Omride wars', *JBL* 85, 441-454.
J.M. Miller 1967	'Another look at the chronology of the early divided monarchy', *JBL* 86, 276-288.
J.A. Montgomery and H.S. Gehman 1951	*A critical and exegetical commentary on the Books of Kings* (I.C.C., Edinburgh).
M. Noth 1957	*Überlieferungsgeschichtliche Studien* (2nd ed., Tübingen, 1957).
J.D. Shenkel 1968	*Chronology and recensional development in the Greek text of Kings* (Harvard Semitic Monographs, vol. 1, Cambridge, Mass.).
E.J. Thiele 1951	*The mysterious numbers of the Hebrew kings: a reconstruction of the chronology of the kingdoms of Israel and Judah* (Chicago, 1951; Exeter, 1966).
S.J. de Vries 1978	*Prophet against Prophet: the role of the Micaiah narrative (1 Kings 22) in the development of early prophetic tradition* (Grand Rapids, Michigan).
M. Weippert 1971	*Edom: Studien und Materialien zur Geschichte auf Grund schriftlicher und archäologischer Quellen* (Tübingen, 1971).
K.H. Bernhardt 1971	'Der Feldzug der drei Könige', *Schalom: Studien zu Glaube und Geschichte Israels* (A. Jepsen Festschrift, ed. K.H. Bernhardt, Stuttgart), 11-22.

MIDIANITES AND ISHMAELITES

Ernst A. Knauf
Institut für alttestamentliche Wissenschaft
und biblische Archäologie
Christian-Albrechts-Universität
Olshausenstr. N 50a
D-2300 Kiel
Federal Republic of Germany

To Frida Stoll - colleague and friend

In Gen. 37:27, we read that Joseph's brothers decide to
sell him to a caravan of Ishmaelites, who had just arrived on
the scene. Midianite traders, however, come along, pull him out
of the cistern, and sell him to the Ishmaelites, who in turn
bring Joseph to Egypt. Gen. 37:36 tells us that the Midianites
sold Joseph to Egypt, but in Gen. 39:1 we read that Potiphar
bought him from the Ishmaelites. Regardless of whether this
text is made up of one or two sources, Midianites and
Ishmaelites, according to Gen. 37, are two different tribes,
both of whom traded between northern Transjordan and Egypt.
Their appearance in central Palestine was apparently nothing
unusual. If the text is made up of two sources, one tribe may
have succeeded the other in this area; if the text derives from
only one source, the two tribes existed at the same time.

In Judg. 8:24, however, the Midianites are said to be
Ishmaelites too, because they wear gold nose-rings /1/. Thus
the two texts clearly contradict each other. In order to
clarify the confusion, we must examine closely all the other
information we have about the Ishmaelites and Midianites.

I

Gen. 25:13-15 lists the tribes of Ishmael. With the
information contained in this document, we can bring together
some of the widely scattered evidence for the individual tribes
of this tribal federation. Some of them are mentioned in the

147

Old Testament by 6th century prophets, in historical
inscriptions of Neo-Assyrian and Neo-Babylonian kings, as well
as in Old South Arabian and Old North Arabian memorial and
dedicatory inscriptions.

On the basis of the dated references and those which we
are able to date, we can conclude that Ishmael probably already
existed as a tribal federation in the central North Arabian and
Syrian desert at the end of the 8th century, was flourishing by
the middle of the 7th century and possibly existed into the 6th
century BC. Later, former groups of the federation, more or
less sedentary, were found on the eastern fringe of the Nile
delta, in southern Palestine, in Transjordan, in the Biqa^c
valley of Lebanon, in Mesopotamia, and in South Arabia.

The Abraham-Hagar-Ishmael narratives (Gen. 16; 21:1-21)
can be explained against the same historical background. There
is no reason to assume the existence of a second tribe of
"Ishmael" in the 2nd millennium BC on the basis of these texts
alone /2/.

II

No extra-biblical evidence is available for the tribe of
Midian. The city, and therefore the land of Midian-Madyan, can
be localized exactly as it has been known under this name into
modern times. It was mentioned and described by classical and
Arab geographers /3/. According to these descriptions, the land
of Midian extended east of the Gulf of ^{c}Aqaba; the city is
certainly identical with one of the fields of ruins at the
present oasis of al-Bad^c in the Wadi l-Abyad /4/. Wadi l-Abyad
runs from north to south, parallel to the coast, and furnished
the only practicable route for traffic in this mountainous
region /5/. Exactly how far the land of Midian extended to the
east and to the south is unclear; the borders probably varied
over the course of time.

According to Gen. 25:4, Midian was divided into five sub-
tribes or districts. Two of them, Elda^{c}a and Hanok, are totally
unknown /6/. The tribal name ^{c}Epher was considered by Musil to
be preserved in the name of Wadi ^{c}Afar (or ^{c}Afal), as the
cultivable part of Wadi l-Abyad below al-Bad^c is called /7/.
We may conclude from this that the ancient capital of Midian
was located in the area of this tribe or district. The biblical
^{c}Epha is certainly identical with the tribe Ḥay(ya)pa mentioned

by the Assyrian kings Tiglath-pileser III and Sargon II /8/.
Perhaps the Ibādidi, another tribe from Sargon's list, can be
identified with the biblical Abīda^c, if both names come from
the root bd^c /9/. There are several place-names in the northern
Hejaz derived from this root /10/. While not mentioned in the
Old Testament, Tamūdi and Mar(')šimani appear in the same
Assyrian list and in texts from classical geographers as
inhabitants of northwest Arabia /11/. On the other hand,
Sargon does not refer to Midian and Epher. It seems highly
improbable to me that the town and the wadi did not exist at
this time. But Midian may have drifted into a 'verkehrsgeo-
graphisches' backwater: it was no longer important for trade in
the 8th century. Epha heads the biblical list, and not Epher,
the tribe of the capital. In Is. 60:6, Epha is mentioned on
equal terms with Midian /12/.

As far as we know, Midian was unimportant in the 1st
millennium BC. But there must have been a time when Midian was
prominent /13/. The time of Midian's flourishing could only
have been the 2nd millennium BC; the reason may have been its
location on the 'incense road'. Midian was most probably
actively engaged in trade. Therefore, the road must have run
through the Wadi l-Abyad. Still in the region of Midianite
influence, it branched off towards Egypt /14/. The Edomite
prince Hadad seems to have made use of this branch of the road
when he fled from Edom to Egypt via Midian and Pharan /15/
(1 Kgs. 11:18). At the time of Sargon II, however, the road
seems to have shifted further inland, perhaps following the
route of the present-day Hejaz Railway /16/. I think the reason
for this shift in routes lies in the history of the camel.

III

As R.W. Bulliet has proved, it is impossible to give an
exact dating for the domestication of the camel, as it was a
process which took several hundred years and can be divided into
four stages /17/.

In Stage I, the camel was exclusively a dairy animal, a
sort of 'living capital'. It was rarely used as a beast of
burden, and was never ridden for long distances, as the
extremely impractical pack-saddle belonging to this stage would
indicate (fig. 1). This phase of domestication occurred in the
4th or 3rd millennium BC in southeastern Arabia. The use of
the camel spread thence to southwest Arabia, where it was

developed further, to the island of Socotra, and to the Horn of
Africa, where camel breeding remained restricted to an isolated
area and was untouched by new developments of domestication.

The transition to stage II occurred in West Arabia,
probably before 2000 BC. The people living along the 'incense
road' began to use the camel as a beast of burden /18/. The
haulānī-saddle (fig. 2) was then developed to provide more
comfort for riding over long distances. Yet still, the saddle
was not suited for warfare. Since the merchandise carried on
the 'incense road' had a high value but was small in quantity,
only small caravans with few animals would have been necessary.
The haulānī-saddle became popular throughout Arabia, and is
still in use in South Arabia.

In stage III - the proto-bedouin stage /19/ - nomads
attempted to use the camel for military purposes, and developed
the cushion-saddle (fig. 3), which enabled the rider to fight to
a limited extent with bow and arrow (fig. 4). Proto-bedouins
as well as bedouins rode camels in battle and were organized in
large tribes. For the proto-bedouins, however, the camel was
only part of their stock, and they were unable to use a lance
or a sword while riding their camels. The earliest evidence for
this stage of domestication is found in 1 Sam. 30:17, in a
relief from Tell Halāf (9th century BC: fig. 3) and in the
Assyrian report on the battle of Qarqar (853 BC), in which an
Arab chieftain with 1000 camels is mentioned as one of the
protagonists. This 'proto-bedouin' stage began no later than
1000 BC /20/, the centre of innovation probably being North
Arabia. The Ishmaelites belong to this stage.

The fourth and final stage in the history of camel
domestication took place with the bedouins. They emerged
somewhere between 500 and 200 BC in North Arabia; the Arabs
participating in the battle of Magnesia (198 BC) used the
šadād-saddle /21/. This saddle (fig. 5) enabled them to fight
with lance or sword while mounted on the camel. Such 'camel-
fighting' was, of course, useful only for attacking and
defending caravans (fig. 6). Still, this development was to
change the balance of power in the heart of Arabia /22/.
Warriors mounted on camels, however, never stood a chance in
a pitched battle against a well-trained infantry.

The rerouting of the 'incense-road' to the east prior to
the 8th century /23/ is due, I think, to the transition from

stage II of camel domestication to stage III in this part of
Arabia. Use of the camel as a means of transportation passed
from the sedentary, agricultural town-dwellers of West Arabia
to the proto-bedouins. Dependent herders became independent
tribes, and trade routes were established in their grazing areas.

The Midianites of the late Bronze and early Iron Age lived
along the 'incense road' and participated in the trade passing
along it. The camel played only a subsidiary role in their
economy. The archaeological evidence as well as the place
names themselves, which have in part been retained till today,
would tend to indicate that the Midianites were a sedentary,
agricultural society, employing terrace farming and other
irrigation techniques in their wadis /24/. The so-called
'Hejaz pottery' may serve as an additional argument, since
bedouins would have no use for such breakable objects /25/.

IV

Why, then, did the Midianites carry out raids into
Palestine at the beginning of the Iron Age? Even if the
narrative in Judg. 6-8 was written much later than the events
described, the facts are still much too anchored in tradition /26/
to be completely unfounded. I can only suggest the following
hypothesis: with the breakdown of Syrian-Aegaean culture at the
end of the Bronze Age, trade also succumbed /27/. The out-of-
work Midianite traders employed the camel, their means of
transportation, to transport men instead of merchandise, to
take by force what they could not gain by trade. The raiding
parties were apparently small. According to the most ancient
strata of the Gideon tradition /28/, only the men of Gideon's
own clan, some 300, participated in his fights. There are
latter day parallels for such long distance raids. In March
1908, a division of the Ḥuwēṭāt, a tribe composed primarily of
farmers and breeders of goats and sheep who occupied the
territory of ancient Midian /29/, raided Salamiya near Hamā in
Syria /30/. The use of the camel as a means of transportation
explains the extensive Midianite activities at that time. This,
however, does not yet make them bedouins.

Only one passage in the Old Testament, Judg. 6:1-5, depicts
the Midianites as nomads who invade the land with immense herds
and devastate it. This passage, however, belongs to the
editorial framework of the book of Judges and probably was not
written before the 6th century /31/. At this time, the

inhabitants of Palestine had already had plenty of opportunity
to become acquainted with another type of camel-rider.
According to Assyrian accounts, Qedar, a tribe of Ishmael,
raided the countries west of the Arabian peninsula "again and
again". In the middle of the 7th century, the king of Moab
managed to drive them back /32/. One hundred years later,
however, there was no king of Moab, no king of Ammon, and no
king of Judah any more. There was no military power which could
have prevented the proto-bedouins from raiding anywhere they
wanted /33/. Judg. 8:24 ("For they had golden earrings, because
they were Ishmaelites") is most probably a gloss, but the
glossator is completely correct. The historiographer of the
exilic or post-exilic period used the Ishmaelites, with whom he
was acquainted, as a model for his depiction of the Midianites.
These "Midianites" were indeed Ishmaelites.

V

Midianites and Ishmaelites had nothing to do with each
other in terms of their way of life, the geographical areas
they occupied, or the time at which they flourished. How they
ended up side-by-side in the Joseph narrative is a problem in
the history of ancient Hebrew literature /34/, not a problem of
the history of North Arabia in the Late Bronze and Iron Age.

NOTES

Mrs. Margaret M. Clarkson, Tübingen, and Mrs. Lesley Gansel,
Kiel, improved greatly upon my English style. H. Donner, Kiel,
and H.G. Rothe, Tübingen, read an earlier draft of this paper
and contributed most helpful criticism. Arabic place and tribal
names are transliterated according to the written form.

/1/   Or "earrings"; nose-rings are archaeologically attested
for pre-islamic Arabs; cf. Rosenthal (1974), 95f. (Ḥirbat ᶜAbda);
95 n. 2 (Kurnab; nose-ring was found along with earrings); 95
n. 5 (Petra). For nose-rings of earlier times cf. H. Weippert
(1977), 288.
/2/   I have been working on the problem of the Ishmaelites for
some years and hope to present my results - with a documentation
of the complete evidence - in due time; in the meantime, cf.
M. Weippert (1973), 68 n. 113; idem (1977), 172f.

/3/   Cf. Musil (1926), 278-82; in a folk-tale from al-Bad^c
recorded by Burton (1879) I, 164f., "Wadi Madyan" occurs as a
historical name for Wadi Maqa (between al-Bad^c and the Gulf of
^cAqaba). In his days, the country between al-^cAqaba and Muwailiḥ
was still called "Arḍ Madyan", cf. Burton (1878), 104; *idem*
(1879) I, 294f.
/4/   Visited and described by Ruppell (1829), 219f; Burton
(1879) I, 83-111; 136-72; Musil (1926), 108-20; Philby (1957),
211-23; Parr *et al.* (1972), 30-35.
/5/   Cf. Parr *et al.* (1976), 197.
/6/   Ḥnk occurs as a personal name of Safaitic; cf. Harding
(1971), 206. There is no justification for connecting the
Midianite Hanoch with the Cainite (Gen. 4:17f; 5:18) or the
Reubenite (e.g. Gen. 46:9) one. *'Ilda^ca, as far as I know, is
not attested as an Old Arabian personal name as yet, but the
root *d^cw* "to call" is exclusively Arabic and Old South Arabian.
/7/   Cf. Musil (1926), 293; there is, however, a Wadi l-^cIfriya
near Šarma, and a Ǧabal al-Mu^caffara to the south-east of
Maǧayir Šu^caib/al-Bad^c. For ^cfr as an Old Arabian personal and
geographical name, cf. Harding (1971), 425. From Judahite
(1 Chron. 4:17) and Manassite (1 Chron. 5:24) ^cEpher, nothing
can be deduced, the Chronicles being no reliable source for
pre-exilic history.
/8/   ^{uru}ḫa-a-a-ap-pa-a-a K 3751, 3' (Tiglath-pileser III), ed.
M. Weippert (1971), 68; ^{lu}ḫa-ia-pa-a Lyon (1883), pl. 4, 1.20;
Sargon, *Annals* 1.121, ed. Lie (1929), 22. Tiglath-pileser lists
in his document 1.3'-6' the cities and peoples settled along the
'incense road' as far as South Arabia (^{uru}sa-ab'-'-a-a, 1.3'),
thus furnishing the earliest reference to this road (734 BC, cf.
M. Weippert, in press). Sargon, *Annals,* 120-23, claims to have
defeated a group of Arab tribes, and to have deported the
survivors to Samaria. The passage, however, together with a
following note on a tribute received from Egypt, North Arabia,
and South Arabia (1.123-125), is obviously an intrusion into
the narrative of his campaign against Mitā of Muški (1.119f.
125-26). Perhaps an Assyrian vassal or governor met a raiding
party of these tribes, and took some captives, or undertook a
small-scale expedition into North Arabia on his own behalf.
Thus, the date given by the annals, palû 7 = 715 BC, cannot be
trusted. Tadmor (1958), 78, dates this passage to 716 BC, but
his arguments are only valid for 1.123-25. It is not easy to
reconstruct the Arabic name behind the Assyrian transcription.
Biblical ^cĒphā, LXX Gaipha have given rise to the suggestion
*Ǧaifa, but cf. Arabic ǧayyāf "man having a long beard". In
Safaitic, ḥyf and ḥyft are attested; cf. Harding (1971), 232.

If this is the original root, the ^{c}ain in the biblical form may
be due to alliteration with ^{c}Epher. Musil (1926), 289f., thought
^{c}Epha/Ḥay(yā)pa were preserved in the toponym Ruwāfa, which he
transcribes Ṛwāfa (= Ġuwāfa in our system of transcription). I
fear that Musil mistook allophonic velarized rā´(al-mufaḫḫam)
for phonemic ġain. While it is questionable whether the name of
the tribe contained ġain, the name of the place certainly does
not and the identification is to be rejected.

/9/ Abīda^c and Ibadidi were equated, although on the basis of
an untenable philology, by Muṣil (1926), 292. Both names could
be equated, if biblical Abīda^c is popular etymology for an
Arabic 'bd^c , and Assyrian Ibadidi is an error of transmission
for *Ibdādi from *Badādi^c. Note, however, that 'byd^c is a
well-attested Old Arabian personal name (cf. Harding (1971), 18);
*'bd^c is not attested, as far as I know. *Abādid may occur as
Thamudic name (cf. Harding (1971), 10), a 'broken plural', the
singular of which is attested as an Arabic name as well: Abadd
(cf. Caskel (1966) II, 101).

/10/ I happened to note in Musil (1926): al-Bad^c in Wādī l-Abyad;
al-Bad^c, ^{c}Ain al-Bad^c and al-Badī^c in Wādī Dāma (134); Ša^{c}ib
al-Bad^c, al-Badī^c, and a lake al-Bad^c (197); and Badā'i^c in the
far south.

/11/ For references to the tribe of Tamūd, cf. Musil (1926),
291f.; Harding (1971), 148; J.T. Milik in Parr et al. (1972),
54-58; and particularly Graf (1978), 9-12 (although I do not
agree with all of his interpretations and conclusions). The
Mar(')-Šimani (^{Iu}mar-si-i-ma-ni: Lyon (1883), pl. 4 1.20;
^{Iu}mar-si-ma-(ni): Lie (1929), 22.1.121) were equated by Musil
(1926), 292, with the Banizomaneis of Diodorus and Agatharchides
(text. em.) Although his handling of the linguistic problems
involved cannot be justified, his equation seems tenable to me.
I would suggest analyzing Assyrian mar- as Old Arabic *mar',
meaning "son" in most ancient South Arabian (cf. W.W. Müller
in Von Wissmann (1975), 323); later on it came to mean "lord"
(cf. ibid., 370 n.116d), and occurs quite often in Old Arabian
personal names (cf. for example - by no means exhaustive - Knauf
(1980), 171). Thus the replacement of *mar' (coll. sg.) by *banī
may be understood. Interchange of elements of identical or
related meaning in tribal names seems to be quite usual. The
Ḥuwēṭāt Abu Rašid, e.g., became ar-Raša'ida (cf. Von Oppenheim
(1943), 300 with 306 n.7); Āl ^{c}Alī became Wuld ^{c}Ali (cf. ibid.
345). For *Šiman-, cf. Harding (1971), 330 s.v. smn. The
rendering of Old Arabian s$_1$, transcribed s by Harding and others,
by Assyrian written s, spoken š is the normal one; the rendering
of s$_1$ by Greek zeta is unusual, but understandable: in Minaean,
Greek sigma is rendered t, cf. Beeston (1962), 13, para. 7:5.

Obviously, Greek s and Arabian s_1 did not correspond.
/12/ One may ask whether "Midian" was $_c$a geographical name at
this time, denoting the country which Epha inhabited. The
same applies to Hab. 3:7.
/13/ Otherwise, its prominence in Biblical tradition could not
be explained. On the other hand, there is no more information
than this to be derived from the biblical account. These
narratives (Ex. 2:15-4:20; Ex. 18; Num. 25:6-17; Num. 31) are
useless for historical reconstruction. Neither origin nor
transmission of these stories can be pinpointed in space or
time, nor do they refer to persons, places or events that are
mentioned in other, more reliable sources (for Judg. 6-8, cf.
above, section IV). The Midianites in the Balaam-narrative
(Num. 22:4,7) are to be explained as a redactional device to
bridge Num. 22-25 to 31 over the intrusion 26-30; cf. Gross
(1974), 91; Wüst (1975), 216f with n.670. Similarly, Josh.
13:21 is a two-staged gloss, derived in a first stage from
Num. 21:21-30 + 22:2-25:5 + 25:6-17 + 31, giving the extent of
Moses' conquests in the southeast: "whom (sc. Sihon) Moses smote
with the chiefs of Midian, Evi, and Rekem, and Zur, and Hur, and
Reba". A second glossator thought the geographical unity a
political one and interpreted it in this way: "the princes of
Sihon, that dwelt in the land". I hold there is no basis for
the assumption of Eissfeldt (1968), 383-93 and Dumbrell (1975),
323-27, of a Midianite 'league' in the Late Bronze Age, covering
the whole - or the greater part - of North Arabia. It is from
the lists and genealogies, not from the narratives, that we may
expect the biblical writers to give historical information;
cf. Richter (1971), 151f.
/14/ Thus, the older track of the 'incense road' to Syria
should have followed the later pilgrims' route from Egypt; cf.
Musil (1926), 321-26 for the latter. It is generally accepted
that Egypt got most of its incense by sea (cf. Kitchen (1971),
184-207; Müller (1978), 739-41); some, however, may have come by
land via Syria and Arabia; cf. Saleh (1973), 375f, 380f.
/15/ Nowadays, the oasis of Fērān in Wādī Fērān; cf. M. Weippert
(1971), 298r.
/16/ Which followed in turn the pilgrims' route from Syria; cf.
Musil (1926), 326-31. The inland track of the route is attested
for 734 BC by Tiglathpileser III; cf. above n. 8 and Weippert,
in press, with n. 25; for the 5th century BC by Ezek 27:20-22,
cf. Rüger (1961), 109-113; for the 3rd century BC by the Minaean
lists of temple-slaves, ed. Mlaker (1943). For later
attestations of the 'incense road', cf. Müller (1978), 722-34.
/17/ The following remarks are based on Bulliet (1975), 28-110,
with slight modifications concerning the biblical data.

/18/ When the road followed the coast, there were in the wadi
mouths oases enough to have made the route practicable even for
donkey-caravans; cf. Burton (1878), 77, 177f. Even on this
route, however, the camel had an advantage over the donkey,
because the wadi mouths are full of loose sand, "comfortable to
camels and distressing to man and mule" (Burton (1879) II, 87).
/19/ The term "proto-bedouin" was coined by W. Dostal; cf.
e.g. Dostal (1959), 20f.
/20/ According to 1 Sam. 30:17. There were no belligerent
nomads - not to speak of bedouins - to the south of Palestine
prior to the reign of David; cf. the archaeological evidence
presented by Fritz (1980), 121f, 133f, 135.
/21/ Cf. Bulliet (1975), 95.
/22/ Thus, what Caskel (1953) called the "bedouinization of
Arabia" took place several centuries earlier than was assumed
by him; cf. Bulliet (1975), 104.
/23/ Exactly when this process began I cannot say. Was the
settlement of Qurayya an attempt to follow the road inland? The
foundation of the town cannot be dated because of the uncertainty
concerning the time of use of the 'Hejaz Ware'. It required
great skill and experience in irrigation technique, which in all
probability exceeded local knowledge but could have been derived
from Midianite highland settlements. - For Qurayya cf. Moritz
(1923), 29 with pl. 14 (*idem, MUSJ* 3 (1908), 399-415, is at the
moment not accessible to me); Philby (1957), 169-84; Parr *et al.*
(1970), 219-41.
/24/ Cf. Musil (1926), 202 and n. 23 above. A certain amount
of cultural contact, in all probability by trade, between North
Arabia and the Aegean in the Late Bronze Age is attested by the
depiction of a camel on a Mycenaean pot (Late Helladic II
period); cf. Bulliet (1975), 62 with 63, fig. 18.
/25/ Also if one withstands the temptation to connect pots with
peoples, there remains the undeniable fact that in the Late
Bronze/Early Iron Age - and later? - there was ceramic
production on a large scale in North Arabia and it is hardly
conceivable that the Midianites - if they were inhabitants of
this country at this time - did not participate in it. Of
course, there may have existed more than one ethnic entity or
way of life in this territory at this time. But the country of
Midian proper - the wadis of the mountainous region along the
coast - never has been bedouin country in its full sense; cf.
Wallin (1854), 131; Burton (1978), 135.
/26/ Cf. Is. 9:3; Gen. 36:35. Is. 10:26 may depend on Judg. 7:25;
Ps. 83:10-12 presupposes the whole redactional unit Judg. 6-8.
/27/ Cf. Müller-Karpe (1977); Stiebing (1980).

/28/   Cf. Richter (1966), 220-22.
/29/   Cf. Von Oppenheim (1943), 291-97.
/30/   Cf. Musil (1926), 21.
/31/   Judg. 7:12 is a gloss following 6:1-5; cf. Richter (1966),
169.   I cannot agree with Richter (1966), 155, who thinks
6:2b-5 is older than the clearly 'deuteronomistic' verses 1-2a.
Without these, 2b-5 lacks a beginning. Therefore, 2b-5 should
be contemporary or even younger than 1-2a。
/32/   Cf. M. Weippert (1973), 53, 57f; *idem* (1980), 328.
/33/   Cf. Lam. 5:9 "We get our bread with the peril of our
lives/Because of the sword of the wilderness."
/34/   In recent years, there has been much controversy about the
composition, literary character, and dating of the Joseph
narrative; cf. Redford (1970); Meinhold (1975); Donner (1976);
Coats (1976); Seebass (1978); Willi-Plein (1979); Schmitt (1980).
None of these studies, however, is methodologically sound.
Donner (1976) and Willi-Plein (1979) put forward a very
attractive suggestion, but their thesis ought to be controlled
by a literary-critical and form-critical investigation. I do
not agree with their dating.

REFERENCES

BEESTON, A.F.L. *Descriptive Grammar of Epigraphic South
     Arabian* (London, 1962)
BULLIET, R.W. *The Camel and the Wheel* (Cambridge, Mass. and
     London, 1975; 2nd printing, 1977)
BURTON, R.F. *The Gold-Mines of Midian and the Ruined Midianite
     Cities* (1878; edition used: Cambridge/Naples/New York,
     1979)
     The Land of Midian (Revisited), 2 Volumes (London, 1879).
CASKEL, W. "Zur Beduinisierung Arabiens" *ZDMG* 103 (1953),
     28*-36*
     *Ğamharat an-nasab. Das genealogische Werk des Hišam ibn
     Muhammad al-Kalbi,* 2 Volumes (Leiden, 1966)
DONNER, H. *Die literarische Gestalt der alttestamentlichen
     Josephsgeschichte* (Heidelberg, 1976)
DOSTAL, W. "The Evolution of Bedouin Life", *L'antica società
     beduina,* ed. S. Moscati (Rome, 1959), 11-34
DUMBRELL, W.J. "Midian - a Land or a League?" *VT* 25 (1975),
     323-37
EISSFELDT, O. "Protektorat der Midianiter über ihre Nachbarn
     im letzten Viertel des 2. Jahrtausends v. Chr." (1968;
     edition used: *Kleine Schriften* V, Tübingen, 1973, 94-105)
EUTING, J. "Der Kamels-Sattel bei den Beduinen", *Orientalische*

Studien Theodor Nöldeke zum siebzigsten Geburtstag gewidmet ..., ed. C. Bezold (Giessen, 1906), 393-98

FRITZ, V. "Die kulturhistorische Bedeutung der früheisenseitlichen Siedlung auf der Hirbet el-Mšaš und das Problem der Landnahme", *ZDPV* 96 (1980), 121-35

GRAF, D.F. "The Saracens and the Defense of the Arabian Frontier", *BASOR* 229 (1978), 1-26.

GROSS, W. *Bileam. Literar- und formkritische Untersuchung der Prosa in Num. 22-24* (Munich, 1974)

HARDING, G.L. *An Index and Concordance of Pre-Islamic Arabian Names and Inscriptions* (Toronto, 1971)

KITCHEN, K.A. "Punt and How to Get There", *Orientalia* N.S. 40 (1971), 184-207

KNAUF, E.A. "Eine Gruppe safaitischer Inschriften aus der Hesmā", *ZDPV* 96 (1980), 169-73

LIE, A.G. *The Inscriptions of Sargon II, King of Assyria, I: The Annals* (Paris, 1929)

LYON, D.G. *Keilschrifttexte Sargon's Königs von Assyrien (722-705 v. Chr.)* (Leipzig, 1883)

MEINHOLD, A. "Die Gattung der Josephsgeschichte und des Esterbuches: Diasporanovelle", I *ZAW* 87 (1975), 306-324; II *ZAW* 88 (1976), 72-93

MLAKER, K. *Die Hierodulenlisten von Ma^{c}in* (Leipzig, 1943)

MORITZ, B. *Arabien. Studien zur physikalischen und historischen Geographie des Landes* (Hanover, 1923)

MÜLLER, W.W. *Weihrauch. Ein arabisches Produkt und sein Bedeutung in der Antike* (Munich, 1978: offprint from Pauly-Wissowa, Supplement XV)

MULLER-MARPE, H. "Zum Ende der spätkanaanitischen Kultur", *Jahresbericht des Instituts für Vorgeschichte der Universität Frankfurt a.M. 1976* (1977), 57-77.

MUSIL, A. *The Northern Hegaz* (New York; 1926)

OPPENHEIM, M. Freiherr von, *Die Beduinen, II: Die Beduinenstämme in Palästina, Transjordanien, Sinai, Hedjaz* (Leipzig, 1943)

PARR, P., HARDING, G.L., DAYTON, J.E. *Preliminary Survey in N.W. Arabia, 1968, BIAUL* 8-9 (1970), 193-242; 10 (1972), 23-61

PHILBY, H.St.J. *The Land of Midian* (London, 1957)

REDFORD, D.B., *A Study of the Biblical Story of Joseph (Genesis 37-50)* (Leiden, 1970)

RICHTER, W., *Traditionsgeschichtliche Untersuchungen zum Richterbuch* (2nd edition, Bonn, 1966)
Exegese als Literaturwissenschaft. Entwurf einer alttestamentlichen Literaturtheorie und Methodologie (Göttingen, 1971)

ROSENTHAL, R. "A Nabataean Nose-Ring from Avdat (Oboda)",
    IEJ 24 (1974), 95-96.
RÜGER, H.P. *Das Tyrusorakel Ez 27* (Diss. ev. theol., Tübingen,
    1961)
RUPPELL, E. *Reisen in Nubien, Kordofan und dem peträischen*
    Arabien, vorzüglich in geographisch-statistischer
    Hinsicht (Frankfurt a.M., 1829)
SALEH, A. "An Open Question on Intermediaries in the Incense
    Trade during Pharaonic Times", *Orientalia* N.S. 42 (1973),
    370-83.
SCHMITT, H.-C. *Die nichtpriesterliche Josephsgeschichte: ein*
    Beitrag zur neuesten Pentateuchkritik (Berlin/New York,
    1980)
SEEBASS, H. *Geschichtliche Zeit und theonome Tradition in der*
    Joseph-Erzählung (Gütersloh, 1978)
STIEBING, W.H. "The End of the Mycenean Age", *BA* 43 (1980),
    7-21
TADMOR, H. "The Campaigns of Sargon II of Assur: A Chronological-
    Historical Study", *JCS* 12 (1958), 22-40, 77-100
WALLIN, G.A. "Narrative of a Journey from Cairo to Medina and
    Mecca, by Suez, Araba, Tawila, al-Jauf, Jubbé, Hail, and
    Nejd, in 1845", *JRGS* 24 (1854), 115-207
WEIPPERT, H. "Schmuck", *Biblisches Reallexikon,* ed. K. Galling
    (2nd edition, Tübingen, 1977), 282-89
WEIPPERT, M., *Edom. Studien und Materialien zur Geschichte der*
    Edomiter auf Grund schriftlicher und archäologischer
    Quellen (Diss. ev. theol. und Habil.-Schrift, Tübingen,
    1971)
    "Die Kämpfe des assyrischen Königs Assurbanipal gegen die
    Araber" *WO* 7, 1 (1973), 39-85
    "Isamme'", *RLA* V, 3/4 (1977), 172-73
    "Kamāš-ḫaltā", *RLA* V, 5/6 (1980), 328
    "Zur Syrienpolitik Tiglatpilesers III", Paper read to the
    25me Rencontre Assyriologique Internationale, Berlin, 1978
    (in press)
WELCH, S.C. *Persische Buchmalerei* (Munich, 1976)
WILLI-PLEIN, I. "Historiographische Aspekte der Josephsgeschichte",
    Henoch 1 (1979), 305-31
WISSMANN, H. von "Die Geschichte des Sabäerreichs und der Feldzug
    des Aelius Gallus", *Aufstieg und Niedergang der römischen*
    Welt II,9,1 (Berlin/New York, 1976), 308-544
WUST, M. *Untersuchungen zu den siedlungsgeographischen Texten des*
    Alten Testaments, I: Ostjordanland (Wiesbaden, 1975)

FIGURES

Fig. 1   Socotran pack saddle;
after Bulliet (1975), 54 fig. 15.

Fig. 2   South Arabian riding saddle;
after Bulliet (1975), 74 fig. 27.

Fig. 3. Orthostat from
Tell Ḥalāf; after
Bulliet (1975), 82
fig. 33.

Fig. 4 Assyrian
depiction of Arab
camel-riders; after
Bulliet (1975), 83
fig. 34.

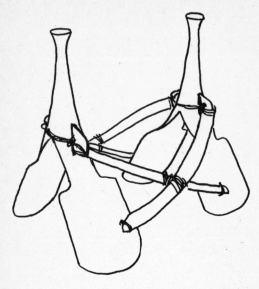

Fig. 5. šadād-saddle; after Euting (1906), 393.

Fig. 6.   Robbers attacking a caravan; from a 16th
century Persian miniature after Welch (1976), pl. 39.

THE MIDIANITE ARC IN JOSHUA AND JUDGES

Elizabeth J. Payne
Department of Religious Studies
University of Newcastle-upon-Tyne

The most common view of Midian is that it was a tribe or confederation of the Late Bronze Age, the settled elements of which occupied territory in the Northern Hijaz, east of the Gulf of Aqaba, whilst its nomadic affiliates could be found pasturing and pillaging in regions as far afield as the Sinai Peninsula in the south and the mountains of Gilead in the north, sometimes invading, on a temporary basis, the agricultural lands of Palestine /1/. The manœuvrability of these nomadic elements has been attributed to the widespread domestication of the camel by the Midianites late in the second millennium BC /2/. This enabled them, it is argued, to conduct raids over hundreds of miles, after the fashion of the more notable razzias /3/.

It is the opinion of the writer, however, that in the period prior to Israel's bid for domination in Palestine, Midianites were actually sedentary in an arc of territory almost surrounding the southern portion of lands held by the Canaanites. According to the texts they are found among groups occupying areas of the Negeb (Num. 10:29ff. with Judg. 1:16; Num. 25:6ff; cf. also the city 'Middin',Josh. 15:61), Edom (I Kgs. 11:18; cf. Hab. 3:3-7), Moab (Gen. 36:35), the Amorite kingdom south of Wadi Zerqa and north of Wadi Mujib (Num. 31:8 with Josh. 13:21; Judg. 8:4ff), the east bank of the Jordan between the Bethshean crossing and Tell Deir ᶜAlla (Judg. 7:22-8:3), the Plain of Jezreel (Judg. 6:1-7:22) and the hills of southern Galilee (Josh. 11:1; Judg. 4:11). As a result of a series of reverses over the following centuries, the Midianite population, which was not absorbed into the new socio-political units of Israel, Judah, Edom and Moab, was pushed back into the deserts of North Arabia. Thus the Assyrian annals of the eighth century BC (ANET, pp. 282, 286) connect some Midianite groups with wealth derived from the carrying of precious commodities from South Arabia to Mesopotamia /4/. The biblical records of the 6th century BC confirm Midianite participation in this lucrative trade,

associating Midian with other well known Arabian merchant groups.
(Gen. 25:1-4; Isa. 60:6f). It is hence no surprise to find in
classical times the mention of towns in the Northern Hijaz which
seem to preserve the ancient name. Josephus refers to "the city
of Madian which lay upon the Red Sea" (*Ant*. 2.257), while
Ptolemy records two towns Μοδιάνα and Μαδιάμα (*Geog*. VII. 2.27)
east of the Gulf of Aqaba. The later association of Midian with
Northern Arabia however does not necessarily confirm that the
tribe occupied this area in either the Late Bronze or Early Iron
Age.

The purpose of this paper is to demonstrate the extent to
which relevant passages of the Books of Joshua and Judges
contribute to our understanding of the northernmost sector of
the "Midianite Arc".

The longest narrative pertaining to Midian, Judges 6-8,
concerns its activity in the Plain of Jezreel, in the Jordan
Valley and in the hills southeast of the Jordan at Damieh, prior
to the establishment of the Israelite monarchy. The situation,
as portrayed by the final form of the texts, is that of a series
of raids on Israel from Transjordanian bases by the allied forces
of the Midianites, Amalekites and People of the East. The main
attacks were concentrated on the Plain of Esdraelon but enemy
activity is even reported "as far as Gaza" (Judg. 6:4). Israel
is liberated from this oppression when the invading forces are
surprised in a night operation by Gideon, a Manassite commander,
beside the Hill of Moreh (Jebel ed-Dahi) in northern Jezreel,
swept off Israelite territory through the combined efforts of
the tribes of Manasseh, Ephraim, Zebulun and Naphtali and finally
defeated by Gideon and three hundred commandos at Karkor in
Transjordan.

It is to the credit of the final editors of this narrative
that so convincing is the portrayal of the Midianites and their
allies as invaders that alternative explanations of Midianite
presence in this area have not been accorded serious consideration.
Commentators have been almost unanimous in their interpretation of
events. The weakening XXth dynasty of Egypt was unable to afford
its customary protection to this strategic region. This initially
enabled incursory Israelite groups to gain a resounding victory
there over the native Canaanite population (Judg. 4-5). Midianite
raiders from east of Jordan were, however, able to take advantage
of the ensuing instability and of their newly acquired mastery of
camel warfare to make a series of devastating harvest-time raids

which threatened to displace the Israelites from their recently appropriated territory /5/.

The first point to be noted against this interpretation is that the "raiding" portrayal is conveyed by relatively few verses (Judg. 6:3-5, 33; 7:12; 8:10aα), and that these statements are clearly part of the editorial framework (Judg. 6:1-2a, 3-6,33,35; 7:12,23; 8:4b, 10aα,b, 28). Outside the editorial material there are no references to the Amalekites as allies of Midian nor any mention of either camels or large numbers of troops. Furthermore, when the work of the final editors is removed, three quite separate conflict sequences emerge. The first describes the expulsion of Midianites from the Plain of Jezreel by Gideon and a small group of Abiezrite clansmen. At the close of this section, in Judg. 7:22, the Midianite refugees have reached the relative safety of the east bank of the Jordan. There is nothing to suggest that Zererah (probably Zarethan), and Abelmeholah, mentioned here as the final destinations of the Midianites, were not themselves Midianite towns. The second sequence seems to have as its basis a Midianite raid from an east bank base on the strategic Ephraimite-held mouth of Wadi Farah (Judg. 7:24-8:3). The allusion in isolation to this battle in Isa. 10:26, where the smiting of Midian at the Rock of Oreb is even compared with the miraculous crossing of the Red Sea, suggests that it originally stood quite independently of the preceding Jezreel narrative. Finally Judg. 8:4ff recounts how a band of Abiezrites conducted a reprisal attack on Midianite Succoth for the murder of a number of their leaders at Tabor in southern Galilee.

The Jezreel narrative, however, once stripped of its editorial material, by no means presents a clear picture of a Midianite foray. Judges 6 rather suggests that the Midianites were inhabitants of the area. After Gideon is called to deliver Israel from the hand of Midian his first act towards that end is to destroy a popular pagan cult in his own town Ophrah. As the angry response of the townsmen suggests (Judg. 6:30), this is hardly the way to raise support for a campaign against the enemy. One explanation of the name Ophrah (Heb. עפרה) might be as a derivative of the name of the Midianite clan Epher (Heb. עפר; Gen. 25:4) /7/, in which case the inhabitants of Ophrah would have been by implication Midianites. This is all the more convincing in the light of 1 Chr. 5:24 which names Epher as a Manassite clan. Epherite presence in this vicinity has already been put forward by W.F. Albright who identified members of the clan with the Apiru which, according to a stele of Seti I (ANET,

p. 255), formed part of the garrison of nearby Bethshean at
that time /6/. Was not then the altar at Ophrah which Gideon
destroyed a Midianite altar?

The implication, if this is so, is that Gideon was himself
a Midianite, since the altar is said to have been under the
custodianship of his father (Judg. 6:11,25). Biblical tradition
connects Moses' Midianite father-in-law with Yahweh prior to the
adoption of that god by Moses' group. Yahwism is also reflected
in the theophoric names of Gideon's family - Joash, his father
(Judg. 6:11, etc.), Jether, a biform of Jethro (cf. Ex. 4:18),
his oldest son (Judg. 8:20) and Jotham his youngest son (Judg.
9:5). The Midianite conflict of Judg. 6:11-7:22 may thus have
arisen out of the championship of Yahwism by one priestly family
within the Midianite sector and its opposition by more
conservative elements of the same group /7/. This could well
have given rise to the slaughtering of Gideon's brothers at the
local sanctuary on Mount Tabor (Judg. 8:18f; cf. Josh. 19:22;
Hos. 5:1). They seem to have been put to death by Midianite
priests of the moon-god, Ṣalm, as is indicated by the name of
one of the murderers, צלמנע (Judg. 8:5ff). Salmunna is almost
certainly a Hebrew play ("protection is withdrawn") on an
original Midianite theophoric name /8/. According to Josephus
(*Ant.* 5.229) Gideon even puts the rival priests to death at
Ophrah. Some vestige of this conflict may also be preserved
in the tradition that Gideon melted down the crescents and
earrings of the spoil, symbols of the cult of the enemy, and
fashioned with them a new image for his sanctuary in Ophrah
(Judg. 8:24-27).

There are additional indications outside the Jezreel
narrative of Midianite possession of this area. In the first
place, a group of Midianite smiths, descendants of Moses' in-
laws, are said to have settled in Galilee (Judg. 4:11) at Kedesh,
identified with Khirbet Qadisa west of the southern end of the
Sea of Galilee (cf. Josh. 19:33). The tale of this clan's
championship of the Yahwistic cause becomes legendary in Israel
(Judg. 4:17-22; 5:6,24-27). Yahwism is also reflected in the
name of the hero of the piece, Jael /9/. This group, however,
have an alliance also with the Canaanites (Judg. 4:17), as do
the inhabitants of the nearby city of Madon (Josh. 11:1),
identified with Qarn Ḥaṭṭin three miles west of Tiberias /10/.
Madon is very likely a dialectical variant of Midian /11/. It
is interesting to note that in connection with this northern
area Medanite and Midianite are used interchangeably (Gen.

37:25-36). Medan appears to be a biform of Madon.

Arabic tradition also testifies to the association of
Midianites with the vicinity of Madon. Barely half a kilometre
from the ruins at Qarn Ḥaṭṭin lies Khirbet Madyan, which name
preserves the consonantal yodh of Midian. Here, according to
local folk legend, is the grave of Shu^ayb, Moses' Midianite
father-in-law /12/.

That the area under attack from Gideon was not an Israelite-
held area is reflected in the Jezreel narrative by the omission
of Issachar from the lists of tribes which gave Gideon
assistance (Judg. 6:35; 7:23). It was in Issachar itself that
the conflict took place (cf. Josh. 19:18); therefore the only
reasonable explanation of the non-cooperation of its tribesmen
with the Israelite forces is that it was not an Israelite but a
Midianite-controlled area. That it is not a chance omission is
demonstrated by the fact that the picture as portrayed in the
biblical texts is consistent. Issachar does not appear in the
list of northern tribes who were unable to drive out the
Canaanites (Judg. 1:22-36). There is no mention of Issachar
when Deborah instructs Barak to gather his men at Tabor, taking
ten thousand from the tribe of Naphtali and the tribe of Zebulun
(Judg. 4:6). This is especially remarkable in view of the fact
that Tabor was an Issacharian cultic place (Josh. 19:22; Dt.
33:18f) but is quite understandable if the sanctuary itself were
under the control of the Midianites of Issachar at that time.
Judg. 5:15, which notes "My princes in Issachar came with
Deborah", also implies that some but by no means all of the
chieftains of that sector could be numbered among the champions
of Yahweh /13/.

It is also suggested in the introduction to the Jezreel
narrative itself that what follows is a description of the
expulsion of a section of the native population from its
holdings. According to Judg. 6:26 the Israelites were living
in camps in the hills, unable, due to Midianite presence, to
penetrate the Plain. There is no suggestion in this strand that
the Israelites had once occupied that area and that they had
been ousted by the Midianites /14/. On the contrary, the
situation is identical to that set out in Josh. 17:16 where the
tribe of Joseph (one element of which was Manasseh) complains
that "the hill country is not enough for us; yet all the
Canaanites who dwell in the plain have chariots of iron, both
those in Bethshean and its villages and those in the Valley of

Jezreel". The Midianites, far from conducting swift razzias, are present with household possessions (*miqneh*) and tents (Judg. 6:5). The trouble they cause as pastoralists results from crop stealing at the expense of neighbouring agriculturalists (Judg. 6:3,11); hence the Israelites are unable adequately to provision their army (Judg. 7:8). The idea that the Midianites swept in to rustle livestock is relatively late, "no sheep or ox or ass" being a gloss on "sustenance" (Judg. 6:4) /15/.

Although the biblical narrative records one successful push against the Midianites of Jezreel by Gideon and the Manassites, the overall picture seems not to have been one of all out victory. According to Judg. 1:27 "Manasseh did not drive out the inhabitants of Bethshean and its villages". That Bethshean, the most important centre of the Plain of Jezreel, did not fall into Israelite hands until at least the time of David is implied by 1 Sam. 31:10ff which recounts that the Philistines were able to display the body of Saul on the city walls there (cf. 2 Sam. 21:12). When Bethshean did eventually become Israelite it was under Manassite not Issacharian control (Josh. 17:11).

The eventual fate of Issachar is alluded to in Gen. 49:14f, where it is stated that he "bowed his shoulder to bear and became a slave at forced labour" (cf. also Judg. 1:27ff). This is usually considered a reference to the enslavement of a section of the Israelite population by stronger Canaanite elements but the situation may well have been quite the reverse. It was perhaps the Midianite population of Issachar which became labourers in the service of the Israelites.

That Midian's Cisjordanian holdings continued into Transjordan is referred to by Gideon in Judg. 7:3 where he calls the battle zone "Mt Gilead" /16/. Midianites fleeing from the initial skirmish make for the relative safety of their territory on the east bank (Judg. 7:22). According to one strand their flight ends in the vicinity of Tabbath (Ras Abu-Tabat near Tell es-Saidiyeh). From the third conflict sequence (Judg. 8:4ff) it seems that Succoth (Tell Deir ^cAlla) was also a Midianite-held settlement from which a contingent had been sent to settle a score at Tabor. Such a territorial continuum was not unknown in later times (cf. Decapolis).

It is also clear from Judg. 8:10ff that the Midianites felt quite at home in the area south of Wadi Zerqa. At Karkor near Jogbehah /17/, that is el-Jubeihat approximately twenty miles

southeast of Damieh, Gideon is said to have caught the Midianite
forces off their guard. Midianite presence in the hill country
south of the Zerqa is also suggested by the fact that Josh. 13:21
names the Midianites as allies of Sihon the Amorite, whose
kingdom extended from the Zerqa to the Mujib (Num. 21:24, Dt.
2:3bff.). According to Num. 31 the major conflict of Israel in
this area in the pre-Conquest times was with Midian rather than
Sihon. Josephus actually refers to this area as "the land of
Midian" (*Ant.* 4.159). This completes the northern sector of the
Midianite Arc extending from the south-Galilean foothills to the
vicinity of Amman.

It remains to discuss why Amalekites and People of the East
should have been introduced into the narrative by the final
editor and why the defeats of sedentary groups should have been
portrayed as the expulsion of raiders.

The Amalekites, normally associated with the deserts to the
south and southeast of Judah, are unlikely to have been the
historical allies of the Midianites so far north. An editor
from the south, however, might have several reasons for including
them here. In the first place, as notorious raiders of the
Negeb, their mention would serve both to bring alive the
narrative for a Judaean audience and to nationalize a local
legend. Secondly, the inclusion of a raiding tribe would add
weight to the overall picture of an incursion by outsiders which
the editor was attempting to create. Similar remarks can be made
concerning the desert dwelling people of the East whose
activities would have been all too familiar to the inhabitants
of eastern Palestine. From Ezek. 25:4,10 it is clear that their
pillaging activities had become proverbial for destruction.
Thirdly, had the editor been influenced by Deuteronomic thought,
he may have wished to see the arch enemy of Israel included in
the narrative (cf. Dt. 25:17-19).

Why then should an editor wish to paint a picture of a
great raid taking place in antiquity? The most probable
explanation is that he wished to create a historical parallel
with the events in his own times.

To which period was the editor referring? Twice in the
eighth century, in 734 BC and 701 BC, huge Assyrian armies had
marched "as far as Gaza" (Judg. 6:4) /18/. No other period of
Judaean history suits the picture better however, than the last
decade of the seventh century BC and the opening years of the
sixth. At this time Judah was surrounded by enemies - to the

north, south and east. In 609 BC Necho's Egyptian army marched
north in support of the floundering Assyrian Empire. 601 BC saw
a reversal with Babylonian troops attacking Egypt via Gaza.
Furthermore the kingdoms of Edom, Moab and Ammon, both at this
time and in the years following, were far from sympathetic to
Judah (Ob. 10-14; Ps. 137:7; Ezek. 25:12; etc.). Judah at this
time was "cornered", so the editor is arguing, just as the
Manassites had once been "cornered" by the Midianites and their
allies. Is the editor, by presenting ancient conflict stories
in this form, where a faithful band drive out oppressors from
every quarter, perhaps holding out some hope of reprieve for
the inhabitants of Judah before the disastrous year of 586 BC?

NOTES

/1/   P. Haupt, "Midian und Sinai", *ZDMG* 63 (1909), 506;
G.M. Landes, "Midian", *IDB*, Vol. 3 (New York, 1962), 375f;
W.J. Dumbrell, "Midian: A Land or a League?", *VT* 25 (1975),
323-337, esp. 327 (this is an abstract from the author's PhD
thesis *The Midianites and their Transjordanian Successors*,
Harvard, 1970); J.P. Hyatt, *Exodus* (London, 1971), 66f; F.M.
Cross, *Canaanite Myth and Hebrew Epic* (Harvard, 1973), 200.
/2/   W.F. Albright, *From the Stone Age to Christianity*
(Baltimore, 1940), 120f; "Midianite Donkey Caravans", in
Translating and Understanding the Old Testament (TUOT), ed.
H.T. Frank and .W.L. Reed (New York, 1970), 197-205. For full
bibliography on the domestication of the camel and related
problems see W.J. Dumbrell's thesis (note 1).
/3/   The application of the Arabic "razzia" (*ghazw*) to the type
of long distance raids which commentators suppose the Midianites
to have conducted (e.g. M.J. LaGrange, *Le Livre de Juges* (Paris,
1903), 119; J.M. Myers, *IB*, Vol. 2 (1953), 683; G.M. Landes,
op. cit., 376) betrays a misunderstanding of the specialized
meaning of the term. The anthropologist L.E. Sweet has
demonstrated that it specifically applies to "reciprocal"
raiding within Bedouin culture but may not be used to designate
"unilateral" raiding directed against non-Bedouin tribes or
communities ("Camel Raiding of the North Arabian Bedouin: A
Mechanism of Ecological Adaptation", *The American Anthropologist*
67 (1965), 1132-50).
/4/   F. Delitzsch first suggested the identification of the
Ḫaiappa of the annals of Tiglath-Pileser III and Sargon II with
the Midianite tribe of Ephah (Gen. 25:4; Is. 60:6) (*Wo lag das
Paradies? Ein biblischassyriologische Studie* (1881), 304). See

also his *Die Keilinschriften und das A.T.* (3rd ed., Zimmern and Winckler, 1902) 58; E. Meyer, *Die Israeliten und ihre Nachbarstämme* (Halle, 1906), 317.

A. Musil connected Ephah with Rwâfa (Rawâfa, Ghwafah), a site in the Central Hisma, approximately 75 km SSW Tebuk (*The Northern Heğaz* (New York, 1926), 184f). Musil also identified Abida, Midian's fourth son (Gen. 25:4), with the Ibadidi of the records of Sargon II (*ibid*. 292; cf. *ANET*, 286). This name has been associated with the oasis of Badᶜ, on the east of the Gulf of Aqaba near the mouth of the W. Afal (recently, see F.V. Winnett, "Arabian Genealogies of the Book of Genesis", in *TUOT* (see note 2), 192; J. Van Seters, *Abraham in History and Tradition* (New Haven and London, 1979), 61).

/5/   Some examples of this view: G.F. Moore, *A Critical and Exegetical Commentary on Judges* (Edinburgh, 1895), 173; A. Musil, *op. cit.*, 261; A. Malamat, "The War of Gideon and Midian: A Military Approach", *PEQ* 85 (1953), 61; Y. Kaufmann, *The Biblical Account of the Conquest of Palestine* (Jerusalem, 1953), 81, 87; J.M. Myers, *op. cit.*, 683; C.A. Simpson, *The Composition of the Book of Judges* (Oxford, 1957) 25; J. Gray, *Archaeology and the O.T. World* (London, 1962), 125; R. de Vaux, *Histoire Ancienne d'Israël. La Période des Juges* (Paris, 1973), 119ff; J.D. Martin, *The Book of Judges* (Cambridge, 1975), 79.

A slightly different complexion on events is cast by G.E. Mendenhall who supposes that non-Semitic migrants from Anatolia and N. Syria superimposed themselves upon a native Semitic population to give rise to the Midianite group which is confronted in the biblical texts. The migrant population brought with them the domesticated camel and hence the possibility of a completely new lifestyle in the areas in which they settled (*The Tenth Generation* (Baltimore and London, 1973), esp. 108-119, 163-73). R.G. Boling endorses this view (*Judges* (New York, 1975), 122).

/6/   W.F. Albright, "The Jordan Valley in the Bronze Age", *AASOR* VI (1924-5), 35f (a view later withdrawn).

/7/   This would provide supportive evidence for the thesis of N.K. Gottwald that Israel came into existence in Canaan as the result of a successful internal campaign of opposition against the existing Canaanite system, the opposition being identified with the Yahwistic faith (*The Tribes of Yahweh. A Sociology of the Religion of Liberated Israel, 1250-1050 BC* (London, 1980).

/8/   Another example of a Ṣalm name is Ṣalmchezib (G.A. Cooke, *A Text Book of North Semitic Inscriptions* (1903), 195-99) in a fifth century BC Aramaic inscription from Tayma.

/9/   B. Mazar considered that Heber's group perpetuated in
Galilee the Midianite priestly traditions of Moses' kinsmen
("The Sanctuary of Arad and the Family of Hobab the Kenite", *JNES*
24 (1965), 297-303).
/10/   G. Dalman, *Palästinajahrbuch* 10 (1914), 42; W.F. Albright,
AASOR VI (1924-5), 27; *id.*, *BASOR* 29 (1928), 5-6; A. Alt,
Palästinajahrbuch 25 (1929), 50; J. Simons, *GTT* 499; J.A. Soggin,
Le Livre de Josué (Neuchatel, 1970), 104.
/11/   G.E. Mendenhall, *op. cit.*, 165.
/12/   C.R. Conder alludes to this legend (*HDB*, 7th Impression,
Edinburgh, 1909, 202).
/13/   A.D.H. Mayes notes the lack of any reference to Issachar
in the Jezreel narrative "which would have been directly affected
by such a deep incursion into Israelite tribal territory", but
skirts the problem by suggesting, somewhat implausibly, that the
reference to a Midianite encampment in the Plain of Jezreel is
not original ("The Period of the Judges and the Rise of the
Monarch", in *Israelite and Judean History*, ed. J.H. Hayes and
J. Maxwell Miller (London, 1977), 315).
/14/   See recently Martin, *op. cit.*, 79; Boling *op. cit.*, 122.
/15/   Moore, *op. cit.*, 179.
/16/   Several emendations have been put forward including
ויצרפם גדעון and Mt Gilboa or Mt Galud, but there is no necessity
to tamper with the text here.
/17/   Musil's identification of Karkor with Karkar, one of a
group of villages in upper Sirhan known collectively as
Qurayyah al-Milḥ (*op. cit.*, 284), has been widely followed (cf.
recently F.V. Winnett and W.L. Reed, *Ancient Records from North
Arabia* (Toronto, 1970), 59; Boling, *op. cit.*, 156). This
location however seems geographically much too far out of the
picture. The root is common in place-names (cf. Qoraqir in the
North Arabian steppe, Qarqar in Syria) and it is hence
advisable to think of springs or waterholes in the vicinity of
Yogbehah. For this meaning of the root, see J. Gray, *Joshua,
Judges, Ruth* (London, 1967), 310.
/18/   *ANET,* 283f; 287f, respectively.
/19/   For full discussion of this period with reference to the
Babylonian Chronicle see D.J. Wiseman, *Chronicles of the Chaldean
Kings (626-556 BC) in the British Museum* (London, 1956), esp.
15-36.